KAREL the ROBOT

A Gentle Introduction
to the Art of Programming with Pascal

KAREL the ROBOT

A Gentle Introduction
to the Art of Programming with Pascal

Richard E. Pattis
Department of Computer Science
Stanford University

JOHN WILEY & SONS
New York • Chichester • Brisbane • Toronto • Singapore

This book was typeset using the TEX document production system, and camera-ready copy was produced on a CRS Alphatype phototypesetter. Computer resources were provided by the Stanford Artificial Intelligence Laboratory and the Stanford Computer Science Department.

Library of Congress Cataloging in Publication Data:
Pattis, Richard E.
  Karel the robot: a gentle introduction
  to the art of programming.

  Includes indexes.
  1. Electronic digital computers—Programming.
  I. Title.
QA76.6.P38   001.64'2   80-26748
ISBN 0-471-08928-1

20 19 18 17 16

To the Pattises and Shaffers

PREFACE

KAREL the ROBOT as a Prelude to PASCAL

The first few weeks of a programming course are crucial to the students' perception of the subject; it is during this period that they briefly glimpse the aesthetics of the discipline and are most receptive to new ideas. By starting with Karel the Robot, it will be easy for students to absorb a large number of useful, important, and sophisticated programming concepts quickly. Karel also presents a short, accurate overview of the programming terrain that they will cover again while learning PASCAL. This horizontal slice through the course material allows students to obtain an excellent perspective on the entire programming process.

Many of the advantages of using Karel stem from his programming language, which is entirely imperative. The careful omission of all variables and data structures from Karel's language—except for the data structure that represents the state of Karel's world—immediately allows this text to introduce and explore thoroughly the simpler, yet still rich domain of abstraction and control structures. Using this approach, students can plunge into programming and problem solving while incurring a minimum of overhead. They quickly learn to write well-structured programs (with potentially interesting bugs) instructing Karel to perform complicated tasks.

The time spent learning Karel's programming language will pay for itself repeatedly during the PASCAL course. The major abstraction and control structures of PASCAL are covered in this book, as are the concepts of rigorous syntax and BEGIN/END block structuring. Common syntactic and semantic pitfalls are highlighted, and a healthy dose of programming rules and homilies is thrown in for good measure, encouraging students to adopt good programming habits early in the course. Because of the designed-in similarities, PASCAL will be much easier to learn after students have become familiar with Karel's robot programming language.

Many important programming ideas can be studied only after covering large portions of a programming language, whether the language is Karel's or PASCAL. By using this text, significant concepts are covered once at the beginning of a programming course, and then they can be reviewed and reinforced while the students learn PASCAL.

Another pro-Karel argument addresses the "fear of computing" syndrome. Many students have a dread fear of anything that is associated with computers, especially in domains that are also numerical in nature (unfortunately, computers and numbers seem inexorably linked). I have even found this attitude prevalent among science and engineering majors. As a result, I believe that programming fundamentals are best taught in a world that is more intuitive, easier to understand, and less hostile than the world of computers.

Students are much more adept at designing and visualizing Karel's programs, which move a robot through the streets of a city, than they are with computer programs, which move information through the circuits of a computer. The confidence that they gain while studying Karel will promote a calmer approach toward the study of PASCAL. But do not be misled by the apparent simplicity of Karel and his world; although Karel's world is quite restrictive—a definite advantage when teaching the fundamentals of programming—there still is adequate room for complex behavior. (In fact, Karel's computational power is equivalent to that of a Turing machine.)

Finally, students must acquire a vocabulary of technical terms in order to think and speak accurately about programming. I have tried to help students obtain this requisite vocabulary by identifying and reasonably naming common programming concepts. A hefty number of these technical terms are defined and repeatedly used throughout this book.

The Mechanics of Using <u>KAREL the ROBOT</u>

<u>Karel the Robot</u> is designed to be covered at the beginning of an introductory programming course, prior to the study of a computer programming language.[1] The book has been used at Stanford according to the four day schedule presented below. Although this schedule covers the material at a rapid pace—about 20 pages per class—feedback from students indicates that they do feel comfortable covering the material at this speed.

- Day 1: discuss Chapters 1 and 2, assign students to read Chapters 2 and 3, and assign homework problems from Chapter 2.

- Day 2: discuss homework problems, discuss Chapter 3, assign homework problems from Chapter 3, and assign students to read Chapter 4.

- Day 3: discuss homework problems, discuss Chapter 4, assign homework problems from Chapter 4, and assign students to read Chapter 5.

- Day 4: discuss homework problems, discuss Chapter 5, assign homework problems from Chapter 5, and briefly discuss Chapter 6. (I consider readings and assignments from Chapter 6 optional.)

While studying Karel, my students also familiarize themselves with Stanford's computing facility. These two subjects dovetail when students are asked to prepare portions of their final Karel homework assignment on the text-editing

---

[1]Although this book is intended as an introduction to programming for students progressing to computer programming, it has also been used in computer appreciation classes to illustrate the nature of programming. In addition, this book has been used as a high school text for advanced students, acting as a bridge from BASIC to PASCAL.

system that they will use for composing their PASCAL programs. As a beneficial side effect of this assignment, once students have a machine readable Karel program they have the option of running it on our automatic Karel simulator.

Instructors at Berkeley, who require that their students use the automatic Karel simulator, teach this material (including Chapter 6) on the basis of eight lectures given over a period of two and a half weeks. This style of presentation allows about twice the amount of time to be allotted for each topic. This pacing also allows the simulator to be used as an integral part of learning about Karel. Students are continually given the opportunity to enter, debug, and run their programs on the Karel simulator.

For those instructors and students interested in obtaining and using a Karel simulator, I have written such a program in standard PASCAL. I have tried designing the Karel simulator to provide a simple programming environment that is as gentle to the student as this book aspires to be. Among its features are copious syntactic error messages, a variable-grain trace facility, and completely reversible program execution. Versions exist for both mainframe and microprocessor computer systems. The simulator is being distributed by

Richard E. Pattis
Department of Computer Science
Mail Stop: FR-35
University of Washington
Seattle, WA 98195

Before continuing, I would like to make a short digression and discuss the relative advantages of automatic versus hand simulation of robot programs. I recognize two major merits of automatic simulation: First, the simulator keeps the students totally honest by fully checking their programs for syntactic and execution errors. This immediate reinforcement of programming concepts, relating to both program form and content, is pedagogically desirable. Second, it is fun to watch robot programs run (literally) on a display terminal; students are given a well-deserved pat on the back for developing correct programs.

The main argument against automatic simulation is based on time constraints. If a limited amount of time is available for studying Karel, I suggest that students spend their time reading this book and working the problems, instead of trying to type and debug robot programs. In a time-constrained situation, extensive debugging does not merit the amount of time that it requires. Although this approach does not require the full accuracy of a computer programming language, it does make the students aware of the need for such accuracy.

Finally, there are also advantages inherent in hand simulation. First, it is easy to simulate Karel's programs, because they are totally composed of control structures, without complex arithmetic, input, output, or name bindings. Second, hand simulation is useful when the appropriate hardware is unavailable. But most importantly, hand simulation forces students to demonstrate a total understanding of how a program and a programming language work. Gaining this knowledge is a first critical step toward becoming a competent programmer, and it is important that students recognize this fact.

Proficiency in programming, like many other skills, comes only with practice. Therefore, this book provides problem sets at the end of each chapter, with problems I suggest marked by the "▶" symbol. These selected problems constitute a minimally complete problem set for each chapter. Other problems are provided to allow the instructor and students to substitute for or augment my suggested problems. Most problem sets are ordered in increasing difficulty.

I have included three appendixes that contain references to information that is otherwise diffusely distributed throughout this book. First, **Appendix A** contains a list of the ten built-in robot instructions, as well as information pertaining to the general structure and form of robot programs. Second, technical definitions in this book are underlined for emphasis; **Appendix B** contains a complete list of all underlined terms and the corresponding pages on which they are explained. Finally, since some sections refer to instructions that are defined elsewhere, **Appendix C** contains an index to all the instructions that are defined within this book.

Acknowledgments

Foremost, I would like to thank Brent Hailpern and Marsha Berger for their assistance during the preparation of this book. Both Brent and Marsha were involved in this project from its beginning, and they have given me constant feedback at every stage of the book's development—from high-level think sessions through detailed proofreading. They were enthusiastic supporters of my good ideas, and candid enough to tell me when I was wrong. I greatly appreciate the time that they have shared with me as both colleagues and friends.

I would also like to thank David Wall for what he has taught me about teaching, as well as for his assistance in preparing the figures in this book. John Gilbert and Jim Boyce gave me an invaluable syntactic and semantic critique of my penultimate draft. David Fuchs and Christopher Tucci were instrumental in helping me typeset the preliminary and final versions of this book on the Alphatype. Arthur Keller and Ignacio Zabala provided TEX wizardry.

Karel the Robot has been extensively class tested at Stanford University and the University of California at Berkeley. I have repeatedly received invaluable feedback from the instructors who have used Karel in their courses, and I am doubly indebted to them for giving Karel a chance in their curriculum; therefore, I would like to thank Michael Clancy, Joseph Faletti, Wayne Harvey, Kathy Kronenthal, Mark Tuttle, and Bill Walsh, at Berkeley, as well as Denny Brown, Tom Dietterich, Bob Filman, Mike Kenniston, and Jock Mackinlay at Stanford.

In addition I would like to thank Keith L. Phillips, of the Mathematics Department at New Mexico State University, for critically reading and annotating an earlier draft of this book.

I would be remiss if I did not also acknowledge an intellectual debt owed to Seymour Papert and the MIT LOGO project. Although I have not had any direct contact with this group, except for listening to a few delightful lectures delivered by Dr. Papert, their ideas and research on how to teach programming have had an obvious influence on me.

I would also like to express my gratitude to the staff at John Wiley & Sons—Gene Davenport, Elaine Rauschal, Loretta Saracino, and Rosemary Wellner—for helping me during the publication of this book. They made an inherently difficult process as speedy and painless as possible.

Finally, to housemates Erica Brittain, Anne Crowder, Laura Spivak, and especially Jim Ferrell, I owe my sanity and innumerable apologies for altered dinner schedules.

Richard E. Pattis

CONTENTS

KAREL the ROBOT

A Gentle Introduction
to the Art of Programming with Pascal

CHAPTER ONE

THE ROBOT WORLD

This chapter introduces Karel[1] the robot and sketches the world he inhabits. In later chapters, where a greater depth of understanding is necessary, we shall amplify this preliminary discussion.

1.1 Karel's World

Karel lives in a world that is unexciting by present-day standards (there are no volcanoes, Chinese restaurants, or symphony orchestras), but it does include enough variety to allow him to perform simply stated, yet interesting tasks. Informally, the world is a grid of streets that Karel can traverse. It also contains special objects that Karel can sense and manipulate.

Figure 1–1 is a map illustrating the structure of Karel's world, whose shape is a great flat plane with the standard north, south, east, and west compass points. The world is bounded on its west side by an infinitely long vertical wall extending northward. To the south, the world is bounded by an infinitely long horizontal wall extending eastward. These boundary walls are made of solid *neutronium*, an impenetrable metal that restrains Karel from falling over the edges of his world.

Crisscrossing Karel's world are horizontal <u>streets</u> (running east-west) and vertical <u>avenues</u> (running north-south) at regular, one block intervals. A <u>corner</u>, sometimes referred to as a street corner, is located wherever a street and an avenue intersect. Karel can be positioned on any corner, facing one of the four compass points. Both streets and avenues are numbered; consequently, each corner is identified uniquely by its street and avenue numbers. The corner where 1st Street and 1st Avenue intersect is named the <u>origin</u>.

Besides Karel, there are two other types of objects that can occupy his world. The first type of object is a <u>wall section</u>. Wall sections are also fabricated from the impenetrable metal neutronium, and they can be manufactured in any

---

[1]Karel is named after the Czechoslovakian dramatist Karel Čapek, who popularized the word "robot" in his play <u>R.U.R.</u> (Rossum's Universal Robots). The word "robot" was derived from the Czech word "robota," meaning "forced labor."

desired length. They are positioned sideways between adjacent street corners, effectively blocking Karel's direct path from one corner to the next. Wall sections are used to represent obstacles that Karel must navigate around, such as hurdles and mountains. Enclosed rooms, mazes, and other barriers can also be constructed from wall sections.

The second type of object in Karel's world is a beeper. Beepers are small plastic cones that emit a quiet beeping noise. They are situated on street corners and can be picked up, carried, and put down by Karel. Some of Karel's tasks involve picking up or putting down patterns made from beepers, or finding and transporting beepers.

1.2 Karel's Capabilities

Let's now shift our attention away from Karel's world and concentrate on Karel himself. Karel is a mobile robot: he can move forward, in the direction he is facing, and he can turn in place. He can also perceive his immediate surroundings: Karel posesses a rudimentary sense of sight, sound, direction, and touch.

Karel sees by using any one of his three TV cameras, which point straight ahead, to his left, and to his right. These three cameras are focused to detect walls exactly one half of a block away from Karel. Karel also has the ability to hear a beeper, but only if he and the beeper are on the same corner; the beepers beep that quietly. By consulting his internal compass, Karel can determine which direction he is facing. Finally, Karel is equipped with a mechanical arm that he can use to pick up and put down beepers. To carry these beepers, Karel wears a soundproof beeper-bag around his waist. Karel can also determine if he is carrying any beepers in this bag by probing it with his arm.

Whenever we want Karel to accomplish a task in his world, we must supply him with a detailed set of instructions that explains how to perform the task. Karel is able to receive, memorize, and follow such a set of instructions, which is called a program.

What language do we use to program (here we use "program" to mean "write instructions for") Karel? Instead of programming Karel in English, a natural language for us, we program him in a special programming language, which was designed to be useful for writing robot programs. Karel's robot programming language—like any natural language—has a vocabulary, punctuation marks, and rules of grammar. But this language—unlike English, for example—is simple enough for Karel to understand; yet it is a powerful and concise language that allows us to write brief and unambiguous programs for Karel.

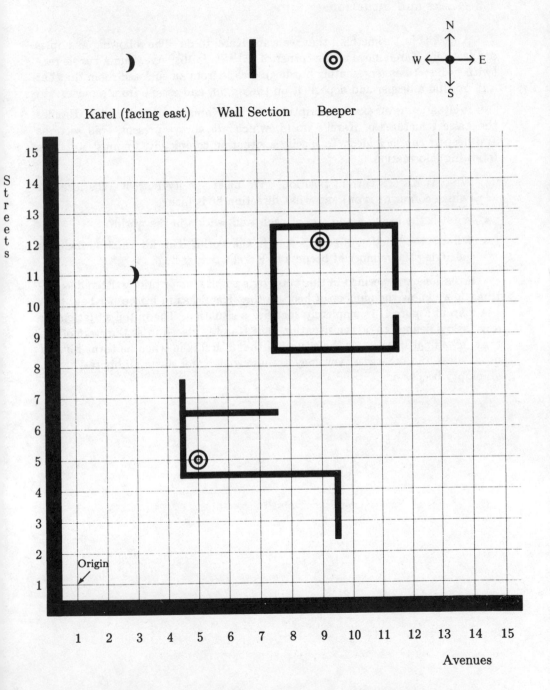

Figure 1–1: The Structure of Karel's World

1.3 Tasks and Situations

A task is just something that we want Karel to do. The following examples
are tasks for Karel: move to the corner of 15th St. & 10th Ave., run a hurdle race
(with wall sections representing hurdles), escape from an enclosed room that has
a door, find a beeper and deposit it on the origin, and escape from a maze.

A situation is an exact description of what Karel's world looks like. Besides
the basic structures of Karel's world, which are always present, wall sections
and beepers can be added. To specify a situation completely, we must state the
following information.

- What is Karel's current position? We must specify both Karel's location
  (which corner he is on) and what direction he is facing.

- What is the location and size of each wall section in the world?

- What is the location of each beeper in the world? This information includes
  specifying the number of beepers in Karel's beeper-bag.

Situations are specified in this book by a small map or brief written description. If we know the number of beepers that Karel has in his beeper-bag, then
the map in Figure 1–1 completely specifies a situation. The initial situation for
any task is defined to be the situation that Karel is placed in at the start of the
task. The final situation is the situation that Karel is in when he turns himself
off. Unless told otherwise, you may assume that Karel starts all his tasks with
an empty beeper-bag.

CHAPTER TWO

PRIMITIVE INSTRUCTIONS AND SIMPLE PROGRAMS

This chapter begins our study of Karel's programming language. We shall start with a detailed explanation of the five primitive instructions that are built into Karel's vocabulary. Using these instructions, we can command Karel to move through his world and handle beepers. Section 2.4 demonstrates a complete robot program and discusses the elementary punctuation and grammar rules of Karel's programming language. By the end of this section, we shall be able to write programs that instruct Karel to perform simple obstacle avoidance and beeper transportation tasks.

Before explaining Karel's primitive instructions, we first must define the technical term *execute*: Karel <u>executes</u> an instruction by performing its associated action. Furthermore, Karel executes a program by executing each instruction in the program.

2.1 Changing Position

Karel understands two primitive instructions that change his position. The first of these instructions is **move**, which changes Karel's location.

move   When Karel executes a **move** instruction, he moves forward one block; he continues to face the same direction. To avoid damaging himself, Karel will not move forward if he sees a wall section or boundary wall between himself and the corner that he would move toward. Instead, Karel executes a **move** instruction in this situation by turning himself off. This action, called an *error shutoff*, will be explained further in Section 2.5.

From this definition, we see that Karel executes a **move** instruction by either moving forward (when his front is clear to the next corner) or performing an error shutoff (when his front is blocked). Both situations are illustrated on the next page. Figure 2-1 shows the successful execution of a **move** instruction. The pictured wall section is beyond Karel's one half block range of vision and therefore cannot impede his movement. In contrast, Figure 2-2 shows a thwarted attempt to move. When Karel executes a **move** instruction in this situation, he sees a wall section directly in his path. Relying on his instinct for self-preservation, Karel executes this **move** instruction by performing an error shutoff.

5

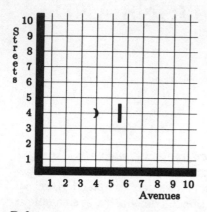
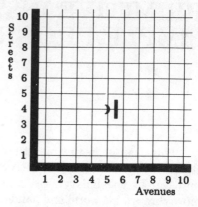

Before move

After move

Figure 2–1: Successful Execution of a move Instruction

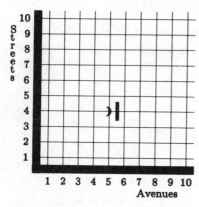
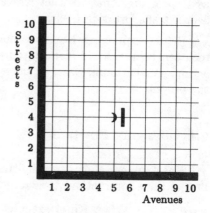

Before move

After move: Error Shutoff

Figure 2–2: Execution of this move Instruction Causes an Error Shutoff

The second primitive instruction that changes Karel's position is turnleft. This instruction changes the direction that Karel is facing, but does not alter his location.

turnleft   Karel executes a turnleft instruction by pivoting 90° to the left; thus, Karel remains on the same street corner while executing a turnleft instruction. Because it is impossible for a wall section to block Karel's turn, turnleft cannot cause an error shutoff.

Karel always starts his task on some corner, facing either north, south, east, or west. He cannot travel fractions of a block or turn at other than 90° angles. Therefore, although both move and turnleft change his position, after executing either of these instructions, Karel still is on some corner and still is facing one of the four compass points.

Karel's designer purposely did not provide him with a built-in turnright instruction. Would adding a turnright to Karel's list of primitive instructions allow him to perform any task he cannot accomplish without one? A moment's thought—and the right flash of insight—shows that the turnright instruction is dispensable; it does not permit Karel to accomplish any new tasks. The key observation for verifying this conclusion is that Karel can manage the equivalent of a turnright instruction by executing three turnleft instructions.

2.2 Handling Beepers

Karel understands two primitive instructions that permit him to handle beepers. These two instructions perform opposite actions.

pickbeeper   When Karel executes a pickbeeper instruction, he picks up a beeper from the corner he is standing on and then deposits it in his beeper-bag. If he executes a pickbeeper instruction on a beeperless corner, Karel performs an error shutoff. On a corner with more than one beeper, Karel randomly picks up one—and only one—of the beepers and then places it in his beeper-bag.

putbeeper   Karel executes a putbeeper instruction by extracting a beeper from his beeper-bag and placing it on his current street corner. If Karel tries to execute a putbeeper instruction with an empty beeper-bag, he performs an error shutoff.

Beepers are so small that Karel can move right by them; only wall sections and boundary walls can block his movement.

2.3 Finishing a Task

Finally, we need a way to tell Karel that he is finished with his task. The turnoff instruction fulfills this requirement.

turnoff   When Karel executes a turnoff instruction, he turns himself off and is incapable of executing any more instructions until he is restarted on another task. The last instruction in every robot program must be a turnoff instruction.

2.4 A Complete Program

In this section we pose a task for Karel and then exhibit a complete program that instructs him to perform the task correctly. Karel's task, illustrated in Figure 2–3, is to transport the beeper from 2nd St. & 4th Ave. to 4th St. &

5th Ave. After he has put down the beeper, Karel must move one block farther north before turning himself off.

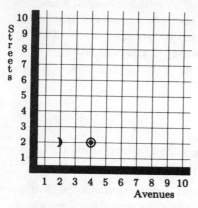

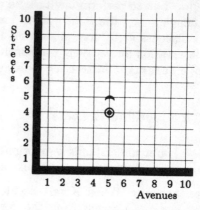

Initial Situation   Final Situation

Figure 2–3: A Beeper Transportation Task

The following robot program correctly instructs Karel to perform this task. The program is constructed from the five primitive instructions, a few new words from Karel's vocabulary, and the semicolon (";") punctuation mark. We'll discuss Karel's execution of this program first, and then we shall analyze the general structure of all robot programs.

```
BEGINNING-OF-PROGRAM
    BEGINNING-OF-EXECUTION
        move;
        move;
        pickbeeper;
        move;
        turnleft;
        move;
        move;
        putbeeper;
        move;
        turnoff
    END-OF-EXECUTION
END-OF-PROGRAM
```

2.4.1 Executing a Program

What must we do to make Karel execute this program? First, we activate Karel by pressing his <u>Turn-On button</u>. Once this is done, Karel's power is switched on, and he is then ready to receive and memorize a program. Next we read Karel the program, making sure to include each word and punctuation mark. In this example, we start by reading: "beginning-of-program beginning-of-execution move semicolon move semicolon pickbeeper semicolon move semicolon turnleft ...." Unfortunately, we cannot communicate the program's indentation to Karel; it is for our benefit only. While we read the program to Karel, he memorizes it, but does not yet start executing the instructions it contains.

When we finish reading the program to Karel, we first set up the initial situation by adding the required wall sections and beepers to the world. Next we press his Execute-Program button, which tells Karel to start executing the program. He is then completely under the control of the program, and we cannot affect his actions again until after he turns himself off. If our program is faulty, we must wait for the error to occur before correcting the program and re-reading it to Karel.

How does Karel execute a program? The rules are quite simple: he sequentially executes each instruction between the words BEGINNING-OF-EXECUTION and END-OF-EXECUTION. This is done, without omitting any instructions, in a strict top to bottom order. Karel continues executing instructions until he either executes a turnoff instruction or performs an error shutoff.

Of course, Karel is not a real robot, so we cannot read him a program and watch him execute it. To determine what a program does, we must *simulate* Karel's execution of it. Simulating a robot program means that we must systematically execute the program exactly as Karel would have, recording every action that takes place. We can hand-simulate a robot program by using markers on a sheet of paper (representing Karel and his world). In order to become proficient robot programmers, we must understand exactly how Karel executes robot programs. The ability to simulate Karel's behavior quickly and accurately is an important skill that we must acquire.

Now we are ready to simulate Karel's execution of our program in the initial situation. We press Karel's Turn-On button, read him the program, set up the world, and press his Execute-Program button. Karel starts executing the program at the **move** instruction directly following the word BEGINNING-OF-EXECUTION. Karel executes this instruction by moving one block east, to 2nd St. and 3rd Ave. Then he executes the next **move** instruction; this causes Karel to move to the same corner as the beeper. Karel successfully executes the **pickbeeper** instruction next. He continues by executing the subsequent **move** instruction, which brings him to the corner of 2nd St. & 5th Ave. Here Karel executes the **turnleft** instruction; this instruction faces him north. He executes the next two **move** instructions, after which he is on the corner of 4th St. & 5th Ave.—where Karel then executes the **putbeeper** instruction. The last **move** instruction directs him one more block northward, to 5th St. & 5th Ave. Finally, Karel executes the **turnoff** instruction, completing the program and accomplishing the required task. Thus, we have verified that our program is correct through simulation.

2.4.2 The Form of Robot Programs

Now that we have a good understanding of how Karel executes a program, let's explore the grammar rules of the robot programming language. Karel pays an inordinate amount of attention to grammar and punctuation rules—a foolish consistency is the hobgoblin of small robot minds—so our time is well spent studying these rules precisely. We start by dividing the symbols that Karel understands into three classes. The first class is punctuation marks, and its only member is the semicolon. All other symbols are in Karel's vocabulary, and they are classified as either instructions, which we have already seen examples of, or reserved words.

Reserved words are used to structure and organize the primitive instructions in Karel's language. Throughout this book, reserved words are printed in upper-case letters, while instructions are printed in lower-case letters. This distinction should help us keep these two word classes separate; only we, however, can benefit from this notation, because Karel only *hears* a program being read—he cannot differentiate between upper-case and lower-case spoken words. In the following discussion, we explain the four reserved words and the punctuation rules used in this programming example. But before proceeding, let's review our program.

```
BEGINNING-OF-PROGRAM
    BEGINNING-OF-EXECUTION
        move;
        move;
        pickbeeper;
        move;
        turnleft;
        move;
        move;
        putbeeper;
        move;
        turnoff
    END-OF-EXECUTION
END-OF-PROGRAM
```

Every robot program must start with the reserved word BEGINNING-OF-PROGRAM. This word is followed by the reserved word BEGINNING-OF-EXECUTION[1], which in turn is followed by a sequence of instructions. After this instruction sequence comes the reserved word END-OF-EXECUTION, finally followed by the reserved word END-OF-PROGRAM. Matching pairs of BEGIN/END reserved words

---

[1]BEGINNING-OF-EXECUTION does not always directly follow BEGINNING-OF-PROGRAM. In the next chapter we shall learn what can be placed between these two reserved words.

are called <u>delimiters</u>, because they delimit the beginning and end of some important entity.

The reserved word BEGINNING-OF-EXECUTION tells Karel where in the program to start executing instructions when his Execute-Program button has been pressed. The reserved word END-OF-EXECUTION does not tell Karel that he is finished executing a program; the turnoff instruction is used for this purpose. Instead, the word END-OF-EXECUTION delimits the end of the instructions that Karel will execute. If Karel is executing a program and reaches END-OF-EXECUTION, it means that a turnoff instruction has been omitted from the program, and Karel will perform an error shutoff. This is an incorrect way for Karel to finish executing a program.

Now let's scrutinize the semicolon punctuation of this program. The semicolon (";") serves to separate consecutive instructions. The rule we must follow is: "Each *instruction* is separated from the next *instruction* by a semicolon." We write each semicolon directly after the first of the two separated instructions. This simple punctuation rule is often misinterpreted as: "Each instruction is followed by a semicolon," but, as we shall see in the next paragraph, these two punctuation rules are slightly different.

The difference between these two punctuation rules can be detected by inspecting the turnoff instruction in the program. The turnoff instruction does not have a semicolon after it because it is followed by END-OF-EXECUTION, which is a reserved word, not another instruction. There is no rule requiring that reserved words be separated from instructions by semicolons. Consequently, whereas the "semicolon after each instruction" rule fails to punctuate this case correctly, the "semicolon between instructions" rule succeeds. Also, notice that two consecutive reserved words, such as BEGINNING-OF-PROGRAM and BEGINNING-OF-EXECUTION, are not separated by a semicolon.

This punctuation strategy is analogous to the way we write a set of numbers in mathematics. For example, we write the set consisting of the elements 1, 4, and 7 as {1,4,7}. In our analogy, the braces are delimiters, the numbers are instructions, and the commas between numbers take the places of semicolons. If we wrote this set as {1,4,7,}—here we have put a comma after each number; notice the extraneous final comma—it would look as if we had forgotten to write the final number in the set. Likewise, if we included a semicolon after turnoff, Karel would expect to hear another instruction, not the END-OF-EXECUTION reserved word. We must punctuate our programs carefully, as many grammatical errors are the result of incorrect semicolon punctuation.

Finally, notice how delimiters and the entity they delimit are indented. Observe that the entire program is nicely indented, clear, and pleasing to the eye. The importance of adopting a lucid programming style cannot be overemphasized. Embrace the habit not only of writing correct programs, but writing programs that are easy to read. When we discuss different facets of programming style, please pay close attention to these hints and examples, and try to emulate the style of programming presented herein.

Hurrah! You have made it through one of the most fact-packed sections in this book. Much of this material can be learned only through memorization. But take comfort; what appears at present to be a large number of arbitrary conventions and rules will soon seem natural and make logical sense. Programming languages share this arbitrariness with natural languages (why is the thing we sit on called a "chair," and why must a comma precede a conjunction introducing an independent clause?). Take a minute to rest and rejoice before continuing with the next section.

2.5 Error Shutoffs

When Karel is prevented from successfully completing the action associated with a primitive instruction, he executes the erroneous instruction by turning himself off. This action is known as an <u>error shutoff</u>, and its effect is equivalent to Karel's executing a turnoff instruction. But turning off is not the only way such a problem could be addressed: an alternative strategy might have Karel just ignore any instruction that he could not successfully execute. Using this rule he would continue executing the program as if he had never been required to execute the unsuccessful instruction. In the next paragraph, we discuss why Karel's designer chose the first, more conservative of these two options.

To justify this choice, we observe that an error shutoff results from an incorrect program that leads Karel astray. Once an unexpected situation arises— one that prevents successful execution of an instruction—Karel probably will be unable to make further progress toward accomplishing his task. Continuing to execute a program under these circumstances would lead to an even greater discrepancy between what the programmer had intended for Karel to do and what Karel is actually doing; consequently, the best strategy is to have Karel turn himself off as soon as the first inconsistency appears.

So far, we have seen three instructions that can cause error shutoffs: move, pickbeeper, and putbeeper. We must construct our programs carefully and ensure that the following conditions are always satisfied.

- Karel executes a move instruction only when his path is clear to the next corner.

- Karel executes a pickbeeper instruction only when he is on the same corner as at least one beeper.

- Karel executes a putbeeper instruction only when his beeper-bag is not empty.

These conditions are easily met if, before writing our program, we know the exact initial situation in which Karel will be placed. Also, to avoid an error shutoff when a program finishes, we must remember to include a turnoff instruction as the last instruction in our programs.

2.6 Programming Errors

In this section we classify all programming errors into four broad categories. These categories are discussed via an analogy that helps clarify the nature of each error type. You might ask, "Why spend so much time talking about errors when they should never occur?" The answer to this question is that programming requires an inhuman amount of precision, and although errors should not occur *in principle* they occur excessively *in practice*. Instead of expecting to write completely correct programs, we should expect to write 90%-correct programs. We must become adept at quickly finding and fixing errors by simulating our programs. Knowing the names of our enemies is the first step toward defeating them[2], so to this end I dedicate the following discussion.

A lexical error occurs whenever we read Karel a word that is not in his vocabulary. As an analogy, suppose that we are standing on a street in San Francisco, and we are asked by a lost motorist, "How can I get to Portland, Oregon?" If we tell him "fsdt jdhpy hqngrpz fgssj zgr ghhgh grmplhms," we would have committed a lexical error. The motorist is unable to follow our instructions because he is unable to decipher the words of which the instructions are composed. Similarly, Karel must understand each word in a program that he is asked to execute.

Even if Karel recognizes every word in a program, the program still might harbor a syntactic error. This type of error occurs whenever we use incorrect grammar or inaccurate punctuation. Going back to our lost motorist, we might reply, "for keep hundred just miles going eight." Although he recognizes each of these words individually, we have combined them in a senseless, convoluted manner: the parts of speech are not in their correct positions for English grammar. We discussed the grammar rules for basic robot programs in Section 2.4.2.

If our program contains either lexical or syntactic errors, Karel will discover the errors while we read him our program. In both cases, Karel has no conception of *what we meant to say*; therefore, he does not try to correct our errors. Instead, he informs us of the detected errors and then turns himself off, because Karel is incapable of executing a program that he does not fully understand. This action is not an error shutoff, for in this case Karel has no program to execute.

While discussing the next two categories of errors, we shall assume that Karel has found no lexical or syntactic errors in our program. So, after we press Karel's Execute-Program button, he starts to execute the program.

---

[2]In ancient days, a wizard could control an inanimate object by knowing its "true" name. Unfortunately, the true names for programming errors were lost in antiquity, but the "close" names discussed in this section should help us think about finding and fixing errors in our programs.

The third error category is called an <u>execution error</u>. As with lexical and syntactic errors, Karel can also detect these errors when they occur. Execution errors occur whenever Karel is unable to execute an instruction successfully and is forced to perform an error shutoff. Returning to our motorist, who is trying to drive from San Francisco to Portland, we might tell him, "Just keep going for eight hundred miles." But if he happens to be facing west at the time, and takes our directions literally, he would travel for only a few miles before reaching the Pacific Ocean. At this point he would stop, realizing that he cannot follow our instructions to completion. Likewise, Karel will turn himself off if he is asked to execute a primitive instruction that he is incapable of completing successfully.

The final error class is the most insidious, because Karel cannot detect this type of error when it occurs. We label this category of error an <u>intent error</u>. An intent error occurs whenever Karel successfully completes his program, but does not successfully complete his task. This means that the program is incorrect for the task, but not so incorrect that Karel can discover the error. Coming back to our motorist, we could again tell him, "Just keep going for eight hundred miles." If this time he happens to be facing south, he can successfully follow our instructions to completion, but he will end up in Tijuana, Mexico.

Remember that Karel does not *understand* the task for which we have programmed him; all Karel knows is how to execute the instructions we have given him in our program. Thus, there is no way for him to know that the program did not accomplish what we intended.

Frequently, intent errors occur early in a program and later lead to execution errors. Once Karel makes a wrong turn or moves incorrectly, it is only a matter of time before he tries to move through a wall or pick up a beeper that is not where he thinks it should be. Therefore, just because an instruction causes an error shutoff, it does not mean that the instruction is wrong; an earlier incorrect instruction might lead to an error that Karel discovers later in the program. In such cases, we must trace backward through the program from the instruction that caused the error shutoff, to discover which instruction started Karel on his errant path. This type of interaction, between intent and execution errors, is illustrated concretely in Problem 2.7–1.

2.6.1 Bugs and Debugging

In programming jargon, all types of errors are known as <u>bugs</u>. There are many apocryphal stories about the origin of this term. In one story the term "bug" is said to have been originated by telephone company engineers. They used the term to describe the source of random noises transmitted by their electronic communications circuits, saying that there were bugs in the circuits.

In another story, the Harvard Mark I computer was producing incorrect answers. When the engineers took it apart, trying to locate the problem, they found that a dead fly (which was caught between the contacts of a relay) was causing the malfunction; ergo, the first computer bug. Other stories abound, so perhaps we shall never know the true entomology of this word.

The term "bug" became popular in programming to save the egos of programmers who could not admit that their programs were full of errors. Instead, they preferred to say that their programs had bugs in them. Actually, the metaphor is apt: bugs are hard to find, and although a located bug is frequently easy to fix, it is difficult to ensure that all bugs have been found and removed from a program. Debugging is the name that programmers give to the activity of removing errors from a program.

2.7 Problem Set

The purpose of this problem set is to test your knowledge of the form and content of simple robot programs. The programs you are required to write are long, but not complicated. Concentrate on writing grammatically correct, pleasingly styled programs. Refer back to the program and discussion in Section 2.4 for rules and examples of correct grammar and punctuation. Verify that each program is correct by simulating Karel in the appropriate initial situation.

▶1. Start Karel in the initial situation illustrated in Figure 2–4 and simulate his execution of the program below. Karel's task is to find the beeper, pick it up, and then turn himself off. Draw a map of the final situation, stating whether an error occurs. If an execution or intent error does occur, explain how you would correct the program. This program has no lexical or syntactic errors.

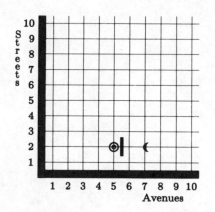

Figure 2–4: Initial Situation for Problem 1

```
BEGINNING-OF-PROGRAM
  BEGINNING-OF-EXECUTION
    move;
    turnleft;
    turnleft;
    move;
    turnleft;
    move;
    turnleft;
    move;
    pickbeeper;
    turnoff
  END-OF-EXECUTION
END-OF-PROGRAM
```

▶**2.** Carefully inspect the following program and correct all lexical and syntactic errors. **Hint:** There are eight errors: five errors involve semicolons, one is grammatical, and the other two errors are lexical. Confirm that each word is in an appropriate place and that it is a correctly spelled instruction name or reserved word. You may use the program in Problem 2.7–1 as a model for a lexically and syntactically correct program.

```
BEGINNING-OF-EXECUTION;
  BEGINNING-OF-PROGRAM
    move;
    move
    pickbeeper;
    move;;
    turnleft;
    move;
    move;
    turnright;
    putbeeper;
    move;
    turnoff;
  END-OF-EXECUTON
END-OF-PROGRAM;
```

3. What is the smallest, lexically and syntactically correct Karel program?

4. Every morning Karel is awakened in bed when his newspaper, represented by a beeper, is thrown onto the front porch of his house. Program Karel to retrieve his paper and bring it back to bed with him. The initial situation is given in Figure 2–5, and the final situation must have Karel back in bed (same corner, same direction) with the newspaper.

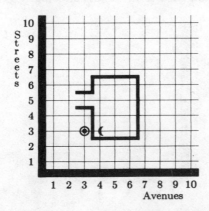

Figure 2–5: Initial Situation for the Newspaper Retrieval Task

▶5. The wall sections in Figure 2–6 represent a mountain (north is up). Program Karel to climb the mountain and then plant a flag, represented by a beeper, on the summit; Karel then must descend the other side of the mountain. Assume that he starts with the flag-beeper in his bag. Remember that Karel is not a super-robot from the planet Krypton who can leap to the top of the mountain, plant the flag, and then jump down in a single bound (his name is Karel, not Kar-el). As illustrated, Karel must closely follow the mountain's face on his way up and down.

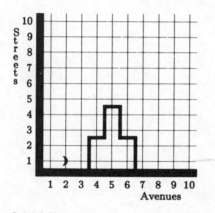
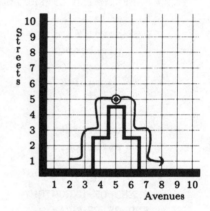

Initial Situation   Final Situation and Karel's Path

Figure 2–6: The Mountain Climbing Task

6. On the way home from the supermarket, Karel's shopping bag ripped slightly at the bottom, leaking a few expensive items. These groceries are represented by—you guessed it—beepers. The initial situation, when Karel discovered the leak, is represented in Figure 2–7. Program Karel to pick up all the dropped items and then return to his starting position.

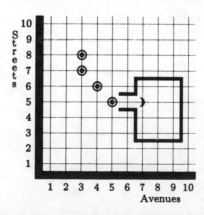

Figure 2–7: Initial Situation for the Grocery Pickup Task

CHAPTER THREE

EXTENDING KAREL'S VOCABULARY

This chapter explains the mechanics of extending Karel's vocabulary and, in the process, discusses the concept of *block structuring*. Besides its usefulness here, block structuring is integrally linked to the other complex instructions that Karel has been built to understand. We shall also demonstrate, in Section 3.8, a style of program construction that is known as *stepwise refinement*. The ability to extend Karel's vocabulary and the method of stepwise refinement complement each other, simplifying our programming problems.

3.1 Creating a More Natural Programming Language

In Section 2.1 we saw that Karel can perform the equivalent of a turnright instruction by executing a sequence of three turnleft instructions. But writing three turnleft instructions for the simple act of turning right is both unnatural and verbose. The robot programming language should contain a more concise way of conveying these instructions to Karel.

Let's look at another clumsy aspect of robot programming. Suppose that we need to program Karel to travel over vast distances. For example, assume that he must move ten miles[1] east, pick up a beeper, and then move another ten miles north. Because Karel understands about moving *blocks* but not *miles*, we must translate our solution into instructions that move Karel one block at a time. This restriction forces us to supply him with a program that contains 160 move instructions. Although the conversion from miles to blocks is straightforward, it results in a very long and unreadable program.

The crux of both these problems is that we think in one language, but must program Karel in another. Rather than make programmers the slaves of the machine, continually forced to translate their powerful ideas into Karel's primitive instructions, Karel's designer turned the tables and endowed Karel with a simple mechanism to *learn* the definitions of new instructions.

Karel's learning ability is actually quite limited. Our programs can furnish him with a *dictionary* of useful instruction names and their definitions, but

---

[1] In Karel's world there are eight blocks to the mile.

each definition must be built from simpler instructions that Karel already understands; the simplest of these instructions are the primitive instructions that Karel intrinsically understands. By providing Karel with instructions that perform complex actions, we can build his vocabulary to correspond more closely to our own. Given this mechanism, we can solve our programming problems using whatever instructions are natural to our way of thinking, and then we can teach Karel the definitions of these instructions.

Returning to our first example, we can inform Karel that the definition of a **turnright** instruction is three **turnleft** instructions. Similarly, we can define a **move-mile** instruction as eight **move** instructions. When Karel must execute either of these new instructions in a program, he remembers the definition associated with the instruction name and executes it. Now our unwieldy beeper-moving program can be written with a **move-mile** definition, containing eight **move** instructions, and another 20 **move-mile** instructions. This program, containing 28 instructions, would be quite an improvement over the original program, which needs 160 instructions to accomplish the task.

More significantly, the smaller program is much easier to read and understand. In complicated problems, the ability to diversify Karel's vocabulary makes the difference between understandable programs and unintelligible ones. We shall detail this extremely important definition mechanism in the next two sections.

3.2 A Mechanism that Defines New Instructions

This section introduces the first component that is needed to define new instructions. Karel's definition mechanism defines a new instruction to have the same meaning as one other instruction. Yes, the learning mechanism is that simple; we can define a new instruction by using only one other instruction that Karel already understands. Concentrate on the upcoming details of this trivial definition mechanism for now, and in the next section we shall discover how to increase its power dramatically. Isolated from a program, the general form of the definition mechanism is given below.

```
DEFINE-NEW-INSTRUCTION <new-name> AS
   <instruction>
```

This mechanism uses the reserved words DEFINE-NEW-INSTRUCTION and AS. The DEFINE-NEW-INSTRUCTION signals Karel that a new instruction is being defined, and AS separates the new instruction name from its definition. When this mechanism is used in a program, we replace <new-name>[2] by any word

---

[2]We use the bracket notation (<new-name> and <instruction>) to help describe Karel's language generally. The word inside the brackets indicates what the bracketed word can be replaced with. For example, we may replace the bracketed word <instruction> by a **move** in one instance and by a **turnleft** in another. **Appendix A** contains a complete list of bracketed words and the associated words in Karel's vocabulary by which they can be replaced.

consisting of lower-case letters and numbers. This word cannot already be the name of an instruction, and we are also prohibited from choosing a reserved word as the name of a new instruction. Despite these restrictions, Karel's language does allow hyphenated names when a multiple-word name is needed (for example, face-north and go-to-wall).

We can replace <instruction> by any single instruction that Karel understands; this instruction becomes the definition of <new-name>. Possible replacements include all of the primitive instructions and any new instructions previously defined by using DEFINE-NEW-INSTRUCTION. Karel executes a new instruction by remembering the definition associated with the instruction's name and then executing it.

The restriction of replacing <instruction> by a single instruction is extremely severe, and it will be rectified in the next section; however, even this simple form of DEFINE-NEW-INSTRUCTION can be useful. If Karel were ever sent to France, his French programmers might employ DEFINE-NEW-INSTRUCTION to create the following simple translations.

```
DEFINE-NEW-INSTRUCTION avance AS
move
```
and
```
DEFINE-NEW-INSTRUCTION tourne-a-gauche AS
turnleft
```

3.3 Block Structuring

When building complex commands such as turnright and move-mile, we frequently need to replace <instruction> by more than just one instruction. Karel's designer chose block structuring as the method to perform this replacement. Block structuring is simple enough for Karel to understand, and it is general enough to be used with other complex instructions in the robot programming language. Block structuring is accomplished by placing a sequence of instructions between the reserved words BEGIN and END, making one big instruction out of a sequence of smaller ones. We write a BEGIN/END block in the following way, using indentation to reinforce the idea that a BEGIN/END block represents one large, aggregate instruction.

```
BEGIN
    <instruction>;
    <instruction>;
      .        .

      .        .

      .        .
    <instruction>;
    <instruction>
END
```

Let's explore the properties of this new grammar rule in greater detail.

- The reserved words BEGIN and END delimit a block whose inside consists of a sequence of instructions separated by semicolons. The internal punctuation of a BEGIN/END block is the same as the internal punctuation of a BEGINNING-OF-EXECUTION/END-OF-EXECUTION block. Remember that a semicolon does not separate the last instruction in the sequence from the reserved word END.

- We can write any number of instructions within a BEGIN/END block—if we want, we may even put in just one. Although a single instruction does not need to be enclosed in a BEGIN/END block, this construction does not violate any of Karel's grammar rules.

- Karel executes a BEGIN/END block by sequentially executing the instructions within the block. Once he starts to execute a BEGIN/END block, Karel eventually executes all of the instructions inside the block, unless he either executes a turnoff instruction or performs an error shutoff.

The fundamental property of a BEGIN/END block is that Karel understands the entire block to represent one instruction. This property permits us to replace <instruction> by a BEGIN/END block. Armed with the concept of block structuring, we can now completely solve the turnright problem by defining the following new instruction. (The move-mile instruction can be written similarly.)

```
DEFINE-NEW-INSTRUCTION turnright AS
BEGIN
    turnleft;
    turnleft;
    turnleft
END
```

So far, we have shown new instruction definitions only outside of a program. In Section 3.5, we shall exhibit a complete program that uses the instruction definition mechanism. But first, we present a slight digression to establish the boundaries of Karel's understanding of new instructions.

3.4 The Meaning and Correctness of New Instructions

Here is an old riddle: "If you call a thumb a finger, how many fingers do you have?" The correct answer is eight, because calling a thumb a finger does not make it one. This riddle is based on the distinction between what a thing *is* and what a thing *is called*. In this section we explore Karel's version of this distinction. In Karel's world, just because you define a new instruction named turnright, it doesn't necessarily mean that the instruction really turns Karel to the right. To demonstrate this point, there are no restrictions prohibiting the following instruction definition.

```
DEFINE-NEW-INSTRUCTION turnright AS
BEGIN
    turnleft;
    turnleft
END
```

According to Karel's rules of grammar, this example is a perfectly legal definition, for it contains neither lexical nor syntactic errors. But by defining turnright this way, we make Karel believe that executing a turnright instruction is equivalent to executing two turnleft instructions. Karel does not *understand* what a turnright instruction is supposed to accomplish; his only conception of a turnright instruction is the definition we give him. Consequently, any new instruction we define may contain an intent error, as the example in this section does.

Besides intent errors, a new instruction can also cause execution errors if it is defined by using primitive instructions that can cause error shutoffs. Can this incorrect definition of turnright ever cause an error shutoff? The answer is no, because turnleft instructions are immune to error shutoffs. As a result, it is impossible for Karel to detect that anything is wrong with this instruction.

This example is somewhat trivial because the error is blatant; but with a more complex defined instruction, we must take care to write a definition that really accomplishes what its name implies. The name specifies *what* the instruction is intended to do; the definition specifies *how* the instruction does what the name implies. The two had better match exactly; otherwise one or both should be changed.

We must also be careful when simulating Karel's execution of a defined instruction. We must adhere to the rule that Karel uses to execute these instructions: Karel executes a defined instruction by executing its definition. Do not try to shortcut this process by doing what the instruction *means*, because Karel does not know what a defined instruction means; he knows only how it is defined. We must recognize the significance of this distinction and learn to interpret Karel's programs as literally as he does.

3.5 Defining New Instructions in a Program

In this section we display a complete robot program that uses the instruction definition mechanism. As in our example of a complete program in the last chapter, we shall first see how the program is executed and then discuss the general form of programs that use this mechanism. Karel's task is shown on the next page in Figure 3–1: he must pick up each beeper in his world while climbing the stairs. Following these maps is a program that correctly instructs Karel to accomplish the task.

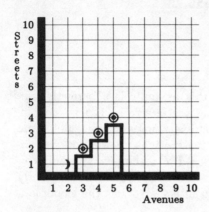

Initial Situation

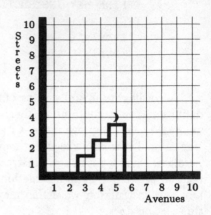

Final Situation

Figure 3–1: A Stair Cleaning Task

```
BEGINNING-OF-PROGRAM
  DEFINE-NEW-INSTRUCTION turnright AS
  BEGIN
    turnleft;
    turnleft;
    turnleft
  END;

  DEFINE-NEW-INSTRUCTION climb-stair AS
  BEGIN
    turnleft;
    move;
    turnright;
    move
  END;


  BEGINNING-OF-EXECUTION
    climb-stair;
    pickbeeper;
    climb-stair;
    pickbeeper;
    climb-stair;
    pickbeeper;
    turnoff
  END-OF-EXECUTION
END-OF-PROGRAM
```

To verify that this program is correct, we simulate Karel's execution of it, emphasizing his execution of the defined instructions. First, we press Karel's Turn-On button and then read him the program. He memorizes the definitions of our two new instructions, turnright and climb-stair, and then he memorizes all of the instructions contained in the BEGINNING-OF-EXECUTION/END-OF-EXECUTION block. Karel finds no lexical or syntactic errors, so, after we have set up the initial situation and pressed his Execute-Program button, Karel starts executing the program at the instruction directly following BEGINNING-OF-EXECUTION.

The first instruction that Karel must execute is climb-stair and, because it is a defined instruction, Karel executes it by remembering and executing its definition. This definition is a BEGIN/END block, which Karel executes by sequentially executing each instruction within the block. He starts to execute this block by first executing the turnleft instruction. After he completes executing this instruction, he executes the move instruction. Karel is then required to execute a turnright. Since the turnright instruction is also defined, Karel executes it by remembering and executing its definition. Thus, Karel next executes the three turnleft instructions that are in the definition of turnright.

After Karel finishes executing turnright, he returns to the climb-stair instruction and executes the final move in its definition. Karel has now completely executed climb-stair and successfully climbed one stair—he is facing east on the same corner as the bottom beeper. Next, because the climb-stair definition has been completely executed, Karel returns to the BEGINNING-OF-EXECUTION/END-OF-EXECUTION block and executes the first instruction after climb-stair, which is the first pickbeeper instruction. This action completes one cycle of the stair cleaning task; Karel executes the other two cycles identically to this one.

Notice that Karel executes climb-stair by remembering and executing its definition. While executing this definition, he is required to execute turnright, which also requires remembering and executing a definition. Karel must temporarily interrupt his execution of the climb-stair instruction to start executing turnright, just as he temporarily interrupted his execution of the BEGINNING-OF-EXECUTION/END-OF-EXECUTION block to execute climb-stair. Karel resumes executing climb-stair after he finishes executing turnright.

It is important for us to understand that no complex rules are needed to execute a program containing defined instructions. Simulating Karel's execution of this program is a bit tedious, because each step is small and simple, but Karel is not equipped to understand anything more complicated. He is able to follow only a very simple, albeit dull, set of rules that tell him how to execute a program. Yet we can use these simple rules, coupled with Karel's willingness to follow them, to command him to perform non-trivial tasks.

We should now understand how Karel executes a program that includes the instruction definition mechanism. We next turn our attention toward program form, and we make the following observations about the stair-cleaning program.

- We briefly mentioned in the previous chapter that something could be written between the BEGINNING-OF-PROGRAM and BEGINNING-OF-EXECUTION reserved words. In our programming example, we saw that the definitions of the two new instructions are placed here. We must always write our new instruction definitions in this area only. We call this portion of the program Karel's <u>dictionary</u>, and each definition is called a <u>dictionary entry</u>.

- The order of instruction definitions is important: Each instruction must be defined before it is used in either a subsequent definition or the BEGINNING-OF-EXECUTION/END-OF-EXECUTION block. In our example, the turnright instruction must be defined first, because turnright is used in the definition of climb-stair. Whenever this order is violated, Karel reports a lexical error—because he will hear an instruction name before he has been told its definition.

- Now on to matters of punctuation, where we introduce two new semicolon punctuation rules. First, observe that dictionary entries are—and must be— separated from one another by a semicolon. Second, the semicolon separating the last dictionary entry from the BEGINNING-OF-EXECUTION/END-OF-EXECUTION block is also necessary.

Karel does not memorize forever the dictionary entries he learns. Each time he is turned on, his vocabulary reverts to the primitive instructions and reserved words that he was originally designed to understand; therefore, each program must contain a complete set of definitions for all new instructions that it uses.

3.6 Boxing: How Karel Understands a Program

In this section we explain how Karel can understand a program by isolating its constituents. The next section and subsequent chapters will demonstrate how we can use this information to help us recognize and avoid common pitfalls when writing and simulating programs. Specifically, in the next section we shall show how Karel can detect a syntactic error (a missing BEGIN/END block in the definition of a new instruction) in a robot program.

We start our study of *boxing* by defining a <u>unit</u> to be either: (1) a primitive or defined instruction name; (2) any type of BEGIN/END block; or (3) a complete dictionary entry. This third type of unit includes the reserved words DEFINE-NEW-INSTRUCTION and AS, the new instruction's name (which is already within its own box by rule 1), and the instruction's definition (which is the first instruction following the AS, and is also already in its own box). In the program on the next page, taken from the previous section, we have drawn <u>boxes</u> around every unit. We call such an operation <u>boxing</u>. By boxing the programs we read to him, Karel is able to check for syntax errors and determine exactly how to execute our programs.

Carefully study the following example to understand how boxing works. To help illustrate the process, the units have been numbered in the order Karel boxes them.

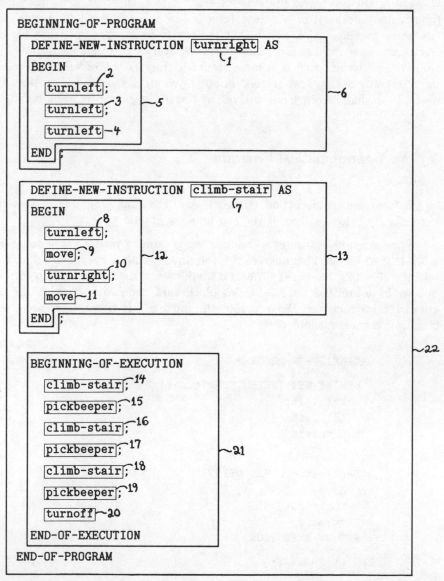

Karel starts boxing a program at its beginning. Generally, he builds units in a top-to-bottom order—but he cannot box a unit until all of its constituents have been boxed. For example, he cannot box a BEGIN/END block until he has boxed all the instructions it comprises. Numerically, each box contains only boxes with smaller numbers. Therefore, within this top-to-bottom order Karel boxes primitive instructions first and then works his way outward, building larger units out of smaller ones.

The main geometric property of boxing is that boxes are either <u>nested</u> (one inside another), or adjacent (one following another). As a rule, units can never overlap. Also, notice that the entire program is itself one big unit. Furthermore, semicolons are placed between every pair of adjacent units. This simple punctuation rule is a more uniform restatement of all the semicolon punctuation rules we have learned in our previous discussions of syntax. From now on, we shall continue our analysis of Karel's grammar by using boxing.

3.7 An Ungrammatical Program

Before reading this section, quickly look at the small program in the example immediately below, and see if you can find a syntactic error.

This program illustrates a common programming mistake: the omission of a BEGIN/END block. The program is nicely indented, but the indentation is misleading. The DEFINE-NEW-INSTRUCTION appears to define turnright correctly, but we have omitted the BEGIN/END block that necessarily encloses the three turnleft instructions. Did you spot the mistake? It is not easy, because the indentation makes it look correct to us.

```
BEGINNING-OF-PROGRAM

   DEFINE-NEW-INSTRUCTION turnright AS
      turnleft;
      turnleft;
      turnleft


   BEGINNING-OF-EXECUTION
      move;
      turnright;
      turnoff
   END-OF-EXECUTION

END-OF-PROGRAM
```

While Karel is being read a program, he continuously checks it for lexical and syntactic errors. Karel discovers syntactic errors by boxing the program and checking for proper grammar and punctuation. In the following example, we illustrate how Karel finds the mistake in our program via boxing. Remember that he only *hears* the program being read and is unaware of our indentation.

```
BEGINNING-OF-PROGRAM
  DEFINE-NEW-INSTRUCTION turnright AS
  turnleft ;
  turnleft;   ?
```

Karel successfully boxes the first unit, turnright, which is the new instruction name. Then he boxes the primitive instruction turnleft that directly follows the AS reserved word. By our omission of a BEGIN/END block, Karel now believes that he has completely boxed the definition of turnright. He also believes that this definition is single turnleft instruction. Karel next boxes the entire dictionary entry, notes the required semicolon, and continues. Then he boxes the next unit, which by the grammar rules must be another definition or the BEGINNING-OF-EXECUTION/END-OF-EXECUTION block. But he finds an inconsistency: this next unit is a turnleft instruction, which does not satisfy either of Karel's options, so he tells us that a syntactic error has occurred. In summary, forgetting to use a necessary BEGIN/END block can lead to syntactic errors.

We are rapidly becoming experts at analyzing programs. Given a robot program, we should now be able to detect grammar and punctuation errors quickly. We should also be able to simulate programs efficiently. But the other side of the programming coin, constructing programs, may still seem a little bit magical. The next section is a first step toward demystifying this process.

3.8 Programming by Stepwise Refinement

This section is a departure from our description of Karel's programming features, and it takes a more general view of programming and problem solving. We shall discuss *stepwise refinement*, a method we can use to construct robot programs. This method addresses the problem of how we can naturally write concise programs that are correct, simple to read, and easy to understand.

It may appear natural to define all the new dictionary entries that Karel will need for a task first, and then write the program using these instructions. But how can we know which new instructions are needed before we write the program? Stepwise refinement tells us first to write the program using any instruction names we desire, and then write the definitions of these instructions. That is, we write the sequence of instructions in the BEGINNING-OF-EXECUTION/END-OF-EXECUTION block first, and then we write the definitions of the new instruction names used within this block. Finally, we assemble all of these separate pieces into a complete program.

We shall explore this process more concretely by writing a program for the task shown in Figure 3–2. These maps represent a harvesting task that requires Karel to pick up a rectangular field of beepers.

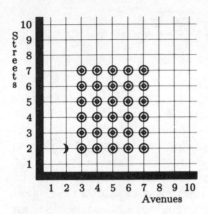

Initial Situation

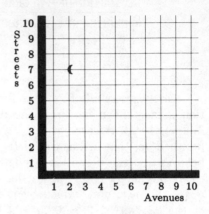

Final Situation

Figure 3–2: The Harvest Task

We program Karel to accomplish this task by commanding him to harvest furrows horizontally, two at a time. Each time he executes the `harvest-2-furrows` instruction, Karel harvests five beepers going east and then comes back west, one block farther north, harvesting five more beepers. He then manuevers into position for harvesting the next two furrows and repeats the entire process two more times. This solution is only one of the many ways we can plan this task; in Problem 3.10–4, you may try writing a program to accomplish this same task by using a different plan. We begin writing the program for this task by translating our basic plan into Karel's programming language.

```
BEGINNING-OF-EXECUTION
    move;
    harvest-2-furrows;
    position-for-next-2;
    harvest-2-furrows;
    position-for-next-2;
    harvest-2-furrows;
    move;
    turnoff
END-OF-EXECUTION
```

We have taken the original task and divided it into several smaller, easier-to-understand subtasks, where each subtask requires us to define a new instruction. Once these subtasks have been solved (all the new instructions have been defined) the original task will also have been solved. So, to continue writing our program, we now must define the new instructions `harvest-2-furrows` and `position-for-next-2`. We write `harvest-2-furrows` first.

```
DEFINE-NEW-INSTRUCTION harvest-2-furrows AS
BEGIN
   harvest-a-furrow;
   go-to-next-furrow;
   harvest-a-furrow
END
```

While writing this definition, we invented two more new instructions to help structure our task, so we add harvest-a-furrow and go-to-next-furrow to the list of instructions that we must eventually define. From this example, we see that stepwise refinement allows our subtasks to generate sub-subtasks. Let's continue with our current train of thought and write harvest-a-furrow first, followed by go-to-next-furrow.

When Karel executes harvest-a-furrow, he must pick up all five beepers in the furrow. Observe that Karel executes this instruction only when he is standing next to the first beeper in a furrow, with the rest of the furrow in front of him. Thus, we can define this instruction directly by using Karel's primitive instructions.

```
DEFINE-NEW-INSTRUCTION harvest-a-furrow AS
BEGIN
   pickbeeper;
   move;
   pickbeeper;
   move;
   pickbeeper;
   move;
   pickbeeper;
   move;
   pickbeeper
END
```

Now we define go-to-next-furrow. Notice that Karel executes this instruction only after harvesting the first of two furrows; therefore, we can assume that he is facing east and wants to go one block farther north and then turn to face west. We also know that when Karel starts to execute this instruction, he is on the corner of the last harvested beeper in a furrow—the easternmost corner.

```
DEFINE-NEW-INSTRUCTION go-to-next-furrow AS
BEGIN
   turnleft;
   move;
   turnleft
END
```

Now we can return to our original plan and write the position-for-next-2 instruction. For reasons similar to those used to write the previous instruction, we know that Karel executes position-for-next-2 only when he is facing west on the corner of the last harvested beeper in a furrow. After Karel executes position-for-next-2, he should be one block farther north and facing east.

```
DEFINE-NEW-INSTRUCTION position-for-next-2 AS
BEGIN
  turnright;
  move;
  turnright
END
```

This leads us back to our old friend the turnright instruction, whose definition is not written here, but must be included in the complete program.

Hey, we're finished! We have defined all the new instructions that we needed to write the program. Now we can assemble these instructions into a complete robot program. Remember that we must ensure that each instruction in the program is defined before it is used. Typically, instructions appear in a program in the reverse of the order in which they were written, with the BEGINNING-OF-EXECUTION/END-OF-EXECUTION block appearing last.

```
BEGINNING-OF-PROGRAM

  DEFINE-NEW-INSTRUCTION turnright AS
  BEGIN
    turnleft;
    turnleft;
    turnleft
  END;

  DEFINE-NEW-INSTRUCTION position-for-next-2 AS
  BEGIN
    turnright;
    move;
    turnright
  END;

  DEFINE-NEW-INSTRUCTION go-to-next-furrow AS
  BEGIN
    turnleft;
    move;
    turnleft
  END;
```

```
DEFINE-NEW-INSTRUCTION harvest-a-furrow AS
BEGIN
  pickbeeper;
  move;
  pickbeeper;
  move;
  pickbeeper;
  move;
  pickbeeper;
  move;
  pickbeeper
END;

DEFINE-NEW-INSTRUCTION harvest-2-furrows AS
BEGIN
  harvest-a-furrow;
  go-to-next-furrow;
  harvest-a-furrow
END;


BEGINNING-OF-EXECUTION
  move;
  harvest-2-furrows;
  position-for-next-2;
  harvest-2-furrows;
  position-for-next-2;
  harvest-2-furrows;
  move;
  turnoff
END-OF-EXECUTION
END-OF-PROGRAM
```

Of course, we should still simulate Karel's execution of this program in the initial situation to verify that it is correct. We may have relied on some invalid assumptions when writing the instructions that move Karel between furrows, or we may have made an error when copying our instructions into the final program. A skeptical attitude toward the correctness of our programs will put us in a good frame of mind for trying to verify them. Programs, unlike United States citizens, are assumed to be guilty of being wrong until they are proven correct.

It is useful to divide a program into many small instructions, even if these new instructions are only executed once. Instruction definitions nicely structure programs, and English words and phrases make programs more understandable; they help convey the intent of the program. As a quick example, we show the basic plan for one solution to Karel's paper-retrieving task, taken from Problem

2.7–4. Although you might have forgotten the task, this program's solution plan
is evident because of the instruction names it uses for subtasks.

```
BEGINNING-OF-EXECUTION
    go-to-door;
    exit-house;
    get-paper;
    return-to-door;
    enter-house;
    go-back-to-bed;
    turnoff
END-OF-EXECUTION
```

Finally, we should always start our stepwise refinements carefully. The early
decisions we make are the most important, as they establish the structure of
the rest of the program. Bad early decisions make it difficult to complete a
program; a good plan, however, will allow the rest of the program refinement
process to proceed smoothly. One way to write a program is to start a few
different refinements, trying different approaches to solving the problem. We
can then review these plans, selecting the best one to use for completing our
stepwise refinement of the program.

This completes our discussion of stepwise refinement in this chapter. In
Section 5.5, we shall construct a more complicated program by again using
stepwise refinement.

3.9 Writing Understandable Programs

Writing understandable programs is as important as writing correct ones;
some say that it is even more important. They argue that most programs initially
have a few errors, and understandable programs are easiest to debug. Good
programmers are distinguished from bad ones by their ability to write clear and
concise programs: programs that someone else can read and quickly understand.
What makes a program easy to understand? We present two criteria.

First, a good program is the simple composition of easily understandable
parts. Each part in our harvesting program can be understood by itself. Even
without a detailed understanding of the parts, the plan that the program uses
to accomplish the complete task is also easy to understand.

Second, dividing a program (or large instruction definition) into small, easy
to understand pieces is not enough. We must also make sure to name our new
instructions properly; these names provide a description of how our program
accomplishes its task (there are typically many different correct programs for
any given task). Imagine what the previous program would look like, if for each
meaningful instruction name we had used a name like first-instruction or

do-it-now. Karel allows us to choose any instruction names we desire, but with this freedom comes the responsibility to select accurate and descriptive names.

It is much easier to verify or debug a program that contains defined instructions. The following two facts support this claim.

- Defined instructions can be independently tested. When writing a program, we should test each instruction immediately after it is written, until we are convinced that it is correct. Then we can forget how the instruction works and just remember what the instruction does. Remembering should be easy, if we name the instruction accurately.

- Defined instructions impose a structure on our programs, and we can use this structure to help us locate bugs. When debugging a program, we should first find which of the defined instructions is malfunctioning. Then we can concentrate on debugging that instruction, ignoring the other parts of our program, which are irrelevant to the bug.

Thus, we see that there is an interesting psychological phenomenon related to Karel's instruction definition mechanism. Because the human brain can focus on only a limited amount of information at any one time, the ability to ignore details that are no longer relevant is a great aid to program writing and debugging.

To help make our new instruction definitions understandable, we should also keep their lengths within a reasonable range. A good rule of thumb is that definitions should rarely exceed five to eight instructions. This limit leaves us enough room to write a meaningful instruction, but restrains us from cramming too much detail into any one definition. If an instruction's size exceeds this limit, we should divide it into a set of smaller instructions. This rule applies to the number of instructions written within the BEGINNING-OF-EXECUTION/END-OF-EXECUTION block too. Most novice programmers tend to write instruction definitions that are too large; resist this temptation. It is better to write many small, well-named instructions, rather than to have a small number of oversized definitions.

In summary, how can writing an understandable program help us? Imagine what the harvesting program would look like if it were written without any defined instructions, using only Karel's primitive instructions. Compare this expanded program with the compact one given in the last section. How easy would it be to convince someone that each is correct? If we made an error by leaving out some part of the program—some single instruction, for example—how easy would it be to locate and correct the error in each case? Finally, if we want to change Karel's task slightly, such as by requiring him to harvest three more beepers per furrow, how difficult would it be to change each of the programs to accomplish this new task? These reasons are part of the overwhelming evidence suggesting that the best program for a task is the one that is the easiest to understand.

3.10 Problem Set

The problems in this section require defining new instructions for Karel, or writing complete programs that include dictionary entries. Concentrate on writing well-structured programs, built from naturally descriptive new instructions. Practice using stepwise refinement and freely define any new instructions that you need. If you find yourself continually writing the same sequence of instructions, it is a sure sign that you need to define that sequence as a new instruction. Carefully check for syntactic errors in your programs, and simulate Karel's execution of each program to verify that it is correct.

Paradoxically, the programs in this problem set will be among the largest you will write. The instructions covered in the next chapters are so powerful that we shall find that complex tasks can be solved with programs comprising a small number of these potent instructions.

▶1. Write appropriate definitions for the following four new instructions: (1) turnaround, which turns Karel around 180°; (2) move-mile, remembering that miles are 8 blocks long; (3) move-backward, which moves Karel one block backward but leaves him facing the same direction; and (4) move-kilo-mile, which moves Karel 1000 miles forward. This last problem is difficult, but a fairly short solution does exist. You may use the move-mile instruction in this problem without redefining it. Also, which of these four instructions might cause an error shutoff when it is executed?

2. Karel sometimes works as a pin-setter in a bowling alley. Write a program that instructs Karel to transform the initial situation in Figure 3–3 into the final situation. Karel starts this task with ten beepers in his beeper-bag.

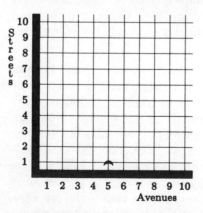

Initial Situation

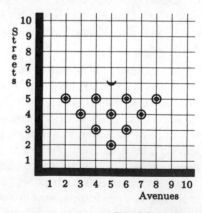

Final Situation

Figure 3–3: A Pin-Setting Task

▶3. Copy the complete program written in the stepwise-refinement section and box it. Make sure that your boxes do not overlap and that semicolons appear only between adjacent boxes.

4. Rewrite the harvesting program using a different stepwise refinement.

▶5. Figure 3–4 illustrates a field of beepers that Karel planted one night when he was drunk after a baseball game. Write a program that harvests all these beepers. **Hint:** This task is not too different from the harvesting example. If you see the correspondence between these two harvesting tasks, you should be able to develop a program for this task that is similar to the original harvesting program.

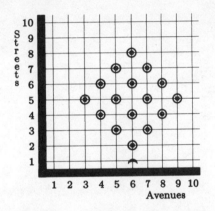

Figure 3–4: Another Harvesting Task

6. Karel wants to send his greetings to the other inhabitants of his universe, so he needs to plant a field of beepers that broadcasts his message to alien astronomers. Program Karel to plant the message of beepers shown in Figure 3–5. You may choose Karel's starting position.

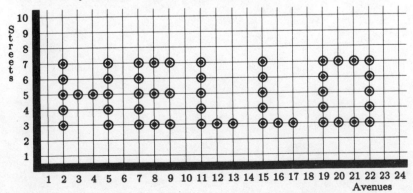

Figure 3–5: A Message for Alien Astronomers

CHAPTER FOUR

CONDITIONALLY EXECUTING INSTRUCTIONS

In the preceding chapters, we always were told exactly which initial situation Karel would be placed in at the start of his task. When we wrote our programs, this information easily allowed us to command Karel to find beepers and avoid running into walls. But these programs were not very general. If Karel tried to execute one in a slightly different initial situation, he would almost certainly be forced to perform an error shutoff. What Karel needs is the ability to survey his local environment and then decide, on the basis of the information he gleans, what to do next.

The IF instructions discussed in this chapter—there are two versions, the IF/THEN and the IF/THEN/ELSE—provide Karel with this decision ability. Both command Karel to test his environment and, depending on the result of the test, allow him to execute an appropriate instruction. These instructions enable us to write much more general programs for Karel—programs that instruct him to accomplish tasks regardless of in which initial situation he is started.

4.1 The IF/THEN Instruction

The IF/THEN instruction is the simpler of the two IF variants, so we shall discuss it first. It has the following general form.

```
IF  <test>
   THEN  <instruction>
```

The IF/THEN instruction introduces the two new reserved words IF and THEN. The reserved word IF signals Karel that an IF instruction is present, and the reserved word THEN separates <test> from <instruction>. The <instruction> is known as the THEN clause of the IF instruction. We indent the IF/THEN instruction as shown, to highlight the fact that the THEN clause is a component of the IF instruction.

Karel executes the IF/THEN instruction by first checking whether <test> is true or false in his current situation. If <test> is true, Karel executes <instruction>; if <test> is false, Karel ignores <instruction>. In either case, he is then finished executing the entire IF/THEN instruction. For an example, let's look at the program fragment[1] below, which consists of an IF/THEN instruction followed by a move instruction (notice the placement of the semicolon between the entire IF instruction and the move instruction).

```
IF next-to-a-beeper
   THEN pickbeeper;
move
```

Karel executes this IF/THEN instruction by first checking whether he is next to (on the same corner as) a beeper. If Karel finds that next-to-a-beeper is true, he executes the THEN clause, which instructs him to execute pickbeeper. He is now finished executing the IF/THEN instruction, and he continues by executing the rest of the program starting at the move instruction.

Now suppose that there are no beepers on the corner when Karel executes this program fragment. In this case <test> is false, so Karel does not execute the THEN clause. Instead, he skips directly to the move instruction and continues executing the program from there. The result of this second case is that Karel executes the IF/THEN instruction by doing nothing more than checking whether he is next to a beeper.

An error shutoff cannot occur in either case, because Karel executes the pickbeeper instruction only if he confirms the presence of at least one beeper on his corner.

4.2 The Conditions Karel Can Test

In Chapter 1 we briefly discussed Karel's sensory modes. We learned that he can see, hear, discover which direction he is facing, and determine if there are any beepers in his beeper-bag. The conditions that Karel can test are divided according to these same four categories. What follows is a complete list of the vocabulary words that can be substituted for the bracketed word <test> in the IF/THEN instruction.

For purposes of classification, Karel treats these words much like primitive instructions; hence, they are written using lower-case letters. Also notice that each condition is available in both its positive and negative form (for example, front-is-clear and front-is-blocked).

- front-is-clear, front-is-blocked,
  left-is-clear, left-is-blocked,
  right-is-clear, and right-is-blocked.

---

[1]To conserve space, we often demonstrate a programming idea without writing a complete robot program or defined instruction. Instead, we just write the necessary instructions, which are called a program fragment.

- next-to-a-beeper and not-next-to-a-beeper.
- facing-north, not-facing-north,
  facing-south, not-facing-south,
  facing-east, not-facing-east,
  facing-west, and not-facing-west.
- any-beepers-in-beeper-bag and no-beepers-in-beeper-bag.

Remember that Karel has three TV cameras for eyes, each focused to detect walls exactly one half of a block away. One camera is facing directly ahead, one is facing toward Karel's left, and the final camera is facing toward Karel's right. He tests right-is-clear, for example, by checking whether there is a wall between himself and the first corner over on his right.

The next-to-a-beeper test is true when Karel is on the same corner as one or more beepers. He cannot hear beepers any farther away, and he obviously cannot hear beepers that are in his soundproof beeper-bag.

Karel consults his internal compass when he must test whether or not he is facing a particular direction.

Finally, Karel can test whether he has any beepers in his beeper-bag by probing it with his mechanical arm.

4.3 Simple Examples of the IF/THEN Instruction

This section examines three instruction definitions that use the IF/THEN instruction. During our discussion of the second definition, we explain what happens when a necessary BEGIN/END block is omitted from a THEN clause. We shall also discuss how IF/THEN instructions are boxed, before concluding.

4.3.1 The harvest-a-furrow Instruction

Do you remember the harvesting task that was programmed in Section 3.8 by stepwise refinement? Karel's new task still requires him to harvest the same size field, but this time there is no guarantee that a beeper is on each corner of the field. Because Karel's original program for this task would cause an error shutoff when it tried to execute a pickbeeper on any barren corner, we must modify it to avoid executing illegal pickbeeper instructions. Karel must harvest a beeper only if he has determined that one is present.

Now that we know about Karel's IF/THEN instruction, we can write a program for this slightly more general task—it is more general because any program that solves the modified harvesting task also solves the original harvesting task. One sample initial situation is illustrated in Figure 4–1.

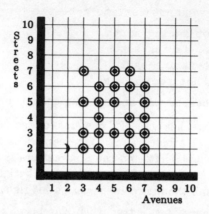

Figure 4–1: A Modified Harvest Task—not all corners have beepers

Please notice that this is only one of many possible initial situations. Our program must be able to harvest this size field (six by five) regardless of which corners have beepers and which corners do not. Luckily for us, almost all of our previously written harvesting program can be reused—another advantage of clear and clean programming. All we need to do is modify the `harvest-a-furrow` instruction by replacing `pickbeeper` with `pickbeeper-if-present`.

```
DEFINE-NEW-INSTRUCTION harvest-a-furrow AS
BEGIN
  pickbeeper-if-present;
  move;
  pickbeeper-if-present;
  move;
  pickbeeper-if-present;
  move;
  pickbeeper-if-present;
  move;
  pickbeeper-if-present
END
```

Of course, we must also write the `pickbeeper-if-present` instruction, but this is easily done by using the IF/THEN instruction.

```
DEFINE-NEW-INSTRUCTION pickbeeper-if-present AS
BEGIN
  IF next-to-a-beeper
    THEN pickbeeper
END
```

Astute grammarians and nitpickers will recognize that the BEGIN/END block surrounding the definition of `pickbeeper-if-present` is superfluous. This block is unnecessary because the definition contains only one instruction—the IF/THEN. The pickbeeper instruction within the THEN clause of this IF is part of the encompassing IF instruction. I shall adopt the convention of always defining a new instruction by enclosing its definition in a BEGIN/END block. I recommend that you too follow this convention, but more importantly, you should know whether such a block is necessary or redundant.

4.3.2 The turnaround-only-if-blocked Instruction

Next we define an instruction that turns Karel around when his front is blocked, but does not change Karel's position when his front is clear. Notice that this definition has a THEN clause whose <instruction> is replaced by a BEGIN/END block. Indeed, Karel's concept of block structuring is useful in IF instructions too. When writing a BEGIN/END block in a THEN clause, we place it beneath the word THEN and indent it two extra spaces to the right.

```
DEFINE-NEW-INSTRUCTION turnaround-only-if-blocked AS
BEGIN
  IF front-is-blocked
    THEN
      BEGIN
        turnleft;
        turnleft
      END
END
```

The BEGIN/END block enclosing this instruction's definition is redundant, because the complete definition is again only one large IF/THEN instruction. However, the BEGIN/END block in the THEN clause is necessary because both turnleft instructions are needed to turn Karel around when his front is blocked. Verify that this instruction is correct by simulating Karel's execution of it.

What happens in this instruction if we accidentally omit the BEGIN/END block in the THEN clause? Study the following *incorrect* definition.

```
DEFINE-NEW-INSTRUCTION incorrect-turnaround-only-if-blocked AS
BEGIN
  IF front-is-blocked
    THEN
      turnleft;
      turnleft
END
```

This instruction may look correct to us; unfortunately, we mere mortals are easily fooled by the instruction's written indentation. Karel is not so stupid—or is it smart? When we read him this instruction, he hears it literally, without indentation information, and boxes it as shown below.

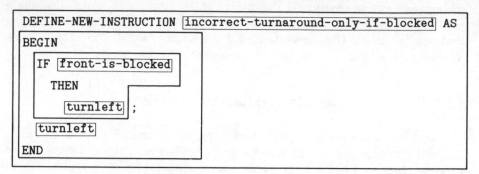

How is this definition different from the correct one? Let's first look at the structural difference between these two instructions. The correct definition consists of one IF/THEN instruction, whose THEN clause is a BEGIN/END block containing two turnleft instructions. The incorrect definition comprises two instructions: the first is an IF/THEN with a turnleft in its THEN clause, and the second instruction is the second turnleft. In the incorrect instruction, this second turnleft is always executed after Karel has finished executing the IF/THEN instruction, regardless of whether his front was blocked or clear.

To show the difference in execution between these two instructions, we simulate Karel's execution of the incorrect definition in a blocked initial situation first and then in a clear one. Whenever Karel's front is blocked, the test will be true; accordingly, he will execute the turnleft instruction that is in the THEN clause. Now that he has finished with the IF/THEN instruction, he executes the second turnleft instruction, which results in Karel being turned around. It is surprising, but in this situation Karel does exactly what we want him to do; however, before assuming that the instruction is correct, we next simulate Karel in a situation where his front is clear. In this case, Karel discovers his front is not blocked when he performs the test, so he skips executing the THEN clause and proceeds to execute the second instruction in the definition—the turnleft. Therefore, when Karel's front is initially clear he does not stay facing the same direction; instead, he turns left.

This simulation demonstrates a subtle intent error. Although we omitted a necessary BEGIN/END block, the resulting instruction is still syntactically correct and, because Karel does not leave his corner during the instruction's execution, this instruction is also immune to execution errors. Furthermore, it even works correctly whenever Karel's front is blocked. But whenever Karel executes this instruction with his front clear, he does not perform the action we intended. What conclusion should we draw from this discussion? To verify that an IF instruction is correct, we must remember to test Karel in all situations that he may encounter while executing the instruction.

It should start to dawn on us that programming errors are indeed possible, and it requires a genuine effort on our behalf to understand the exact meaning of an instruction. Karel determines the meaning of an instruction by boxing it, and we too can use boxing as one way to help us understand an instruction. In addition, a healthy skepticism about the correctness of an instruction is beneficial when we develop test situations to verify that the instruction is correct. An adversary approach is even better suited to this testing phase. Do not passively test an instruction in various situations; instead, actively think of special situations where the instruction may fail to satisfy its intent. Then rigorously simulate Karel in these situations, and determine whether he executes the instruction as we had intended him to execute it.

We end this section with a discussion of one more programming phenomenon related to testing. What might happen if we inadequately test an instruction, assume that it is correct, and use it in a program that Karel executes frequently? Even if we fail to debug an instruction—suppose it is similar to incorrect-turnaround-only-if-blocked in that it works correctly in some situations, but not in others—it may still work correctly in the program for many days, as long as Karel is never asked to execute this instruction in a situation where it does not perform as intended. With each passing day, Karel's programmer will grow more confident that his or her program is correct. But sooner or later, Karel will be required to execute this instruction in an untested-for situation, and then the program may suddenly malfunction.

By this time Karel's programmer will probably have forgotten how the program works, and he or she will have quite a problem finding and fixing the error—especially if the program was poorly written in the first place. From this discussion, we must conclude that there is no guarantee that an inadequately-tested working program will continue to work correctly in the future. This discussion shows why it is so important to verify instructions by testing them in all conceivable situations immediately after they are written.

4.3.3 The face-north Instruction

The final example of an IF/THEN instruction in this section uses Karel's directional abilities. We define face-north, a new instruction that executes by turning Karel to face north regardless of the direction he is initially facing. Observe that if Karel executes this instruction while he is already facing north, the instruction should not turn him at all. Otherwise, he can be turned north by executing at most three turnleft instructions. On the next page we show a defined instruction that accomplishes this task.

Surrounding the definition of this instruction is a mandatory BEGIN/END block, because the definition comprises a sequence of three IF/THEN instructions. In addition, while executing face-north, the only primitive instruction that

Karel can execute is a `turnleft`; therefore, it is impossible for `face-north` to cause an error shutoff.

```
DEFINE-NEW-INSTRUCTION face-north AS
BEGIN
  IF not-facing-north
    THEN turnleft;
  IF not-facing-north
    THEN turnleft;
  IF not-facing-north
    THEN turnleft
END
```

To verify that `face-north` is correct, we must simulate Karel's execution of this instruction in each of four different situations: initially facing north, south, east, and west. We present a detailed simulation for the initial situation where Karel is facing south.

Assuming that Karel is initially facing south, he executes the first `IF/THEN` instruction by determining that the `not-facing-north` test is true. Because <test> is true, he executes the `THEN` clause of the `IF`, which instructs him to turn left. Karel next executes the second `IF` instruction in the sequence that defines `face-north`. He checks the `not-facing-north` test and again finds that it is true (since he is now facing east); therefore, Karel executes the `THEN` clause and again turns to his left. Although Karel is now facing north—the correct direction—he must continue to execute the `IF/THEN` instruction remaining in the `BEGIN/END` block. We shall see that this `IF` instruction does not alter Karel's position further. In the last `IF`, Karel finds that <test> is false and skips the `THEN` clause, completing the definition of `face-north`.

We have now verified that the `face-north` instruction is correct in the initial situation where Karel is facing south. Continue this analysis for the three other possible initial situations to verify that the instruction is completely correct. If we incorrectly wrote the `face-north` instruction by using only two of the three `IF` instructions, which situation(s) would cause the instruction to fail to achieve its intended purpose? If we accidentally included an extra `IF/THEN` instruction in this definition (bringing the total number to four), which situation(s) would cause the instruction to fail to achieve its intended purpose? Check your answers to these questions through simulation.

4.3.4 Boxing the IF/THEN Instruction

Boxing an `IF/THEN` instruction is similar to boxing a dictionary entry, because both use reserved words to separate their different components. Karel boxes an `IF/THEN` instruction by first boxing <test>, then boxing the instruction inside the `THEN` clause (which may be a single instruction or a `BEGIN/END` block), and finally boxing the entire IF/THEN instruction. This last big box includes the reserved words IF and THEN, the previously boxed test, and the previously boxed THEN clause. Study the following example (the numbers again indicate Karel's order of boxing) and the boxing of the incorrect-turnaround-only-if-blocked instruction. Also, study the punctuation in these examples, and try boxing the other instructions that were defined earlier in this chapter.

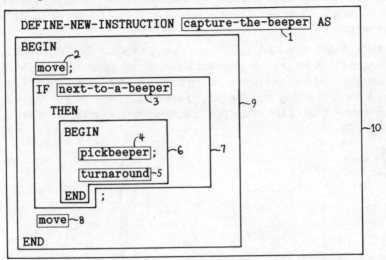

This definition contains three instructions: the first move, the IF/THEN, and the second move. Each of these instructions is separated from the next by a semicolon, and the two instructions inside the BEGIN/END block in the THEN clause are likewise separated by a semicolon.

4.4 The IF/THEN/ELSE Instruction

In this section we discuss the second type of IF instruction that is built into Karel's vocabulary. The IF/THEN/ELSE instruction is useful when, depending on the result of some test, Karel must execute one of two alternative instructions. The general form of the IF/THEN/ELSE is given below.

```
IF  <test>
    THEN  <instruction-1>
    ELSE  <instruction-2>
```

The form of the IF/THEN/ELSE is similar to the IF/THEN instruction, except that it also includes an ELSE clause. Furthermore, the IF/THEN/ELSE instruction can check the same tests as the IF/THEN. Both <instruction-1> and <instruction-2> may be replaced by the same vocabulary words that replace <instruction>. The most common IF/THEN/ELSE punctuation error has a semicolon separating <instruction-1> from the reserved word ELSE; there can be no semicolon placed here. Finally, observe that the THEN and ELSE clauses of this instruction are indented identically.

Karel executes this instruction in much the same manner as an IF/THEN: He first determines whether <test> is true or false in the current situation. If he finds that <test> is true, Karel executes <instruction-1>; otherwise, he finds that <test> is false and executes <instruction-2>. Thus, depending on his current situation, Karel executes either <instruction-1> or <instruction-2>, but not both.

Let's look at a new task that conveniently uses the IF/THEN/ELSE instruction. Suppose that we want to program Karel to run a one mile long hurdle race, where vertical wall sections represent hurdles. The hurdles are known to be only one block high, but they may be placed randomly between any two corners in the race course. One of the many possible race courses for this task is illustrated in Figure 4–2.

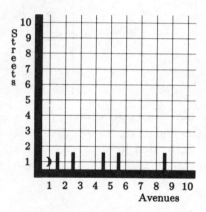 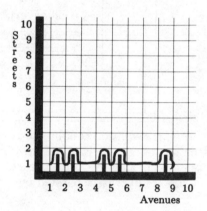

Initial Situation

Final Situation and Karel's Path

Figure 4–2: A Hurdle Jumping Race

Karel could easily run this race by jumping between every pair of corners, but although this strategy is simple to program, it would slow him down too much. Instead, we must program him to move straight ahead when he can, and jump over hurdles only when he must. The program implementing this strategy consists of a BEGINNING-OF-EXECUTION/END-OF-EXECUTION block that contains eight race-stride instructions followed by a turnoff. The definition of race-stride can be written using stepwise refinement.

```
DEFINE-NEW-INSTRUCTION race-stride AS
BEGIN
    IF front-is-clear
        THEN move
        ELSE jump-hurdle
END
```

We continue our refinement by writing jump-hurdle.

```
DEFINE-NEW-INSTRUCTION jump-hurdle AS
BEGIN
  jump-up;
  move;
  glide-down
END
```

Finally, we write jump-up and glide-down, the instructions needed to complete the definition of jump-hurdle.

```
DEFINE-NEW-INSTRUCTION jump-up AS
BEGIN
  turnleft;
  move;
  turnright
END
```

and

```
DEFINE-NEW-INSTRUCTION glide-down AS
BEGIN
  turnright;
  move;
  turnleft
END
```

Of course, the order of these instructions must be reversed in the complete program, and the definition of the omnipresent turnright instruction must also be included. To verify that these instructions are correct, complete and assemble the program, and then simulate Karel's running of the race in Figure 4-2.

4.5 Nested IF Instructions

Although we have seen a large number of IF instructions, we have ignored an entire class of complex IFs. These are known as nested IF instructions, because they are written with an IF instruction nested inside the THEN or ELSE clause of another IF. No new execution rules are needed to simulate nested IFs, but a close adherence to the established rules is required. Simulating nested IF instructions is sometimes difficult because it is easy for us to lose track of where we are in the instruction. The following discussion should be read carefully and understood completely, so that it can be imitated while testing instructions that include nested IFs.

To demonstrate a nested IF instruction, we propose a task that redistributes beepers in a field. This task requires that Karel traverse a field and leave exactly one beeper on each corner. He must plant a beeper on each barren corner and remove one beeper from every corner where two beepers coexist. All corners in this task are constrained to have zero, one, or two beepers on them. One sample initial and final situation is displayed in Figure 4–3. In these maps, multiple beepers on a corner are represented by a number. We can assume that Karel has enough beepers in his beeper-bag to replant the necessary number of corners.

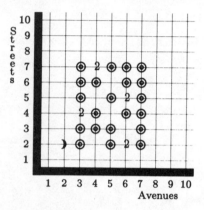
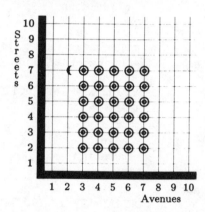

Initial Situation

Final Situation

Figure 4–3: A Beeper Replanting Task

The heart of the program that solves this task is an instruction that satisfies the one-beeper requirement for each corner. We conjecture that the following instruction leaves exactly one beeper on a corner.

```
DEFINE-NEW-INSTRUCTION replant-exactly-one-beeper AS
BEGIN
    IF not-next-to-a-beeper
        THEN putbeeper
    ELSE
        BEGIN
            pickbeeper;
            IF not-next-to-a-beeper
                THEN putbeeper
        END
END
```

This definition has been boxed for easier reading and simulation. The *outside* IF in this definition is an IF/THEN/ELSE and the *nested* IF is an IF/THEN. The nested IF instruction is inside the ELSE clause of the outside IF. Next we simulate Karel in the three possible corner situations: on an empty corner, on a corner with one beeper, and on a corner with two beepers.

In the empty corner situation, Karel executes the outside IF and determines that he is not next to a beeper; therefore, he executes the putbeeper instruction in the THEN clause of the outside IF, placing one beeper on the corner. He has now completely executed the THEN clause of the outside IF instruction, so he is finished executing the outside IF. Because there is only one big IF instruction in this definition, Karel has finished executing replant-exactly-one-beeper, which we have now verified to work correctly in the no-beeper situation.

Next we assume that there is one beeper on Karel's corner. In this case Karel executes the outside IF and finds that the test is false, because he is next to a beeper, so he starts to execute the ELSE clause. This clause is a BEGIN/END block comprising two instructions. First, he executes pickbeeper, picking up the only beeper on the corner. Next Karel executes the nested IF instruction and finds that there are no more beepers on his corner; therefore, he executes the THEN clause of this IF instruction, which commands him to put a beeper back on the empty corner. Karel is now finished with the nested IF, the BEGIN/END block, the entire ELSE clause, the outer IF, and the entire replant-exactly-one-beeper instruction. Thus, Karel also handles the one-beeper situation correctly.

Finally, we assume that Karel is on a corner with two beepers. Here Karel executes the outside IF, finds the test is false, and then executes the ELSE clause. He starts the BEGIN/END block by executing pickbeeper first, picking up one of the two beepers on the corner. At this point Karel has duplicated his actions in the one-beeper situation, but now comes the difference in execution. He executes the nested IF instruction and finds that there still is one beeper on the corner, so he skips the nested IF's THEN clause. Once again Karel is finished with the nested IF, the BEGIN/END block, the entire ELSE clause, the outside IF, and the entire replant-exactly-one-beeper instruction definition. As before, the result is that he has left one beeper on the corner. We have now verified that the replant-exactly-one-beeper instruction is totally correct.

Look back at the boxing and punctuation in this example and notice that there are two END reserved words in succession. This fact accounts for all those instructions and BEGIN/END blocks finishing at the same time. Also, there is only one semicolon in the entire definition. Both of these observations are typical when we deal with instruction definitions containing nested IFs.

Another strategic point worth mentioning is that if nested IF instructions seem too intricate, we should try replacing the nested IF with a new instruction name. The definition of this auxiliary instruction must command Karel to perform the same actions as the nested IF, but the extra level of instruction names may help us better understand what Karel is doing. Because nesting also makes an instruction less readable, a good rule of thumb is to avoid nesting IF instructions more than one level deep. Even in the turnaround-only-if-blocked instruction (which does not contain a nested IF), it is a good idea to define turnaround as two turnleft instructions first and then write turnaround in the THEN clause of the IF. The replant-exactly-one-beeper instruction, which has one level of nesting, is rewritten below, by using an auxiliary instruction.

```
DEFINE-NEW-INSTRUCTION replant-exactly-one-beeper AS
BEGIN
  IF not-next-to-a-beeper
    THEN putbeeper
    ELSE next-to-one-replant-one
END
```

We write the next-to-one-replant-one instruction by copying the ELSE clause from our original definition of replant-exactly-one-beeper.

```
DEFINE-NEW-INSTRUCTION next-to-one-replant-one AS
BEGIN
  pickbeeper;
  IF not-next-to-a-beeper
    THEN putbeeper
END
```

Given the entire program from Section 3.8 along with either of these new definitions of the replant-exactly-one-beeper instruction, do we have a correct solution for the beeper replanting task? We may consider using our old method of verification and test the program with Karel in every possible initial situation, but there are over 200 trillion[2] different fields that this program must be able to replant correctly! It would be ludicrous to attempt verification by exhaustively testing Karel in every possible initial situation.

Instead, we shall settle for probable correctness based on the following informal argument: (1) we have verified that replant-exactly-one-beeper works correctly on any corner that is empty or contains one or two beepers, and (2) we can easily verify that our program commands Karel to execute this instruction on each corner of the field. Therefore, we can combine these two verifications and conclude that the program correctly replants the entire field.

This argument further enhances the claim that Karel's mechanism for instruction definition is a powerful aid to programming. In general, we can informally conclude that an entire program is correct by verifying that: (1) each defined instruction in the program works correctly in all possible situations in which it can execute, and (2) the program executes each defined instruction at the appropriate time. This method allows us to verify a program by splitting it into separate, simpler verifications—just as stepwise refinement allows us to write a program by splitting it into separate, simpler instructions.

---

[2]There are 3 different possibilites for each corner, and there are 30 corners in the field. The total number of different fields is thus 3^{30}, which is 3 multiplied by itself 30 times. For you mathemagicians, the exact number of different fields is $205,891,132,094,649$.

4.6 Transformations for Simplifying IF Instructions

This section discusses four useful transformations that help us simplify programs containing IF instructions. We start by observing that the following two IF/THEN/ELSE instructions, although different in form, execute equivalently. When two instructions result in Karel's performing exactly the same actions, we call this pair of instructions <u>execution equivalent</u>. (For a simple example, one turnleft instruction is execution equivalent to five turnleft instructions—they both leave Karel turned 90° to the left from his original position.)

```
IF front-is-clear          IF front-is-blocked
   THEN move                   THEN jump-hurdle
   ELSE jump-hurdle            ELSE move
```

In general, we can create one execution equivalent IF/THEN/ELSE instruction from another by replacing <test> with its opposite and interchanging the THEN and ELSE clauses. We call this transformation <u>test reversal</u>. Notice that if we perform test reversal twice on the same instruction, we get back to the instruction with which we started.

Test reversal can be used to help novice programmers overcome the following difficulty. Suppose that we start to write an IF instruction and get ourselves into the dilemma illustrated below on the left. The problem is that we want Karel to do nothing special when his front is clear[3], but when his front is blocked we want him to execute <instruction>. We would like to remove the THEN clause, but doing so would cause a syntax error—Karel does not understand an IF/ELSE instruction. The solution to our problem is illustrated on the right.

```
IF front-is-clear          IF front-is-blocked
   THEN do-nothing             THEN  <instruction>
   ELSE  <instruction>
```

To transform the IF on the left into the IF on the right, we use test reversal. First we change <test> to its opposite, then switch the do-nothing instruction into the ELSE clause and bring <instruction> into the THEN clause. By the previous discussion of test reversal, execution equivalence is preserved. Finally, the new ELSE clause (which contains the do-nothing instruction) can be removed, resulting in the simpler IF/THEN instruction on the right.

The second transformation we discuss is <u>bottom factoring</u>. Bottom factoring is illustrated on the next page, where we shall show that the IF/THEN/ELSE instruction on the left is execution equivalent to the program fragment on the right. We have kept the bracketed words in these instructions because their exact replacements do not affect this transformation.

---

[3]We can define the instruction do-nothing as four left turns. Executing this instruction would leave Karel's position unchanged, and this instruction is also immune to error shutoffs.

```
IF  <test>                          IF  <test>
   THEN                                THEN  <instruction-1>
      BEGIN                            ELSE  <instruction-2>;
         <instruction-1>;           <instruction-3>
         <instruction-3>
      END
   ELSE
      BEGIN
         <instruction-2>;
         <instruction-3>
      END
```

In the program fragment on the right, we have *factored* <instruction-3> out of the bottom of each clause in the IF (after factoring, we can remove both redundant BEGIN/END blocks). We justify the correctness of this transformation as follows: If <test> is true, the instruction on the left has Karel execute <instruction-1> directly followed by <instruction-3>.

In the program fragment on the right, if <test> is true Karel executes <instruction-1> and then, having finished the IF, he executes <instruction-3>. Thus, when <test> is true, these forms are execution equivalent. A similar argument holds between the left and right sides whenever <test> is false.

In summary, <instruction-3> is executed in the IF on the left regardless of whether <test> is true or false, so we might as well remove it from each clause and put it directly after the entire IF/THEN/ELSE instruction.

Moreover, if the bottoms of each clause were larger, but still identical, we could bottom factor all of the common instructions and still preserve execution equivalence. Think of this process as bottom factoring one instruction at a time, until all common instructions have been factored. Since execution equivalence is preserved during each factoring step, the resulting program fragment is execution equivalent to the original instruction.

The third transformation we discuss in this section is top factoring. Although this transformation may seem as simple and easy to use as bottom factoring, we shall see that not all instructions can be top factored successfully. We divide our discussion of this transformation into three parts. First, we examine an instruction that can safely be top factored. Then we show an instruction that cannot be top factored successfully. Finally, we state a general rule that tells us which IF instructions can safely be top factored.

Top factoring can safely be used in the following example to convert the instruction on the left into the simpler program fragment on the right. These two forms can be shown to be execution equivalent by a justification similar to the one used in our discussion of bottom factoring.

```
IF facing-north              move;
  THEN                       IF facing-north
    BEGIN                       THEN turnleft
      move;                     ELSE turnright
      turnleft
    END
  ELSE
    BEGIN
      move;
      turnright
    END
```

In the next example, we have incorrectly used the top factoring transformation. We shall discover that the program fragment on the right is not execution equivalent to the instruction on the left.

```
IF next-to-a-beeper          move;
  THEN                       IF next-to-a-beeper
    BEGIN                       THEN turnleft
      move;                     ELSE turnright
      turnleft
    END
  ELSE
    BEGIN
      move;
      turnright
    END
```

To show that these forms execute differently, let's assume that Karel is on a corner containing one beeper, and that the corner in front of him is barren. If Karel executes the instruction on the left, he will first find that he is next to a beeper, and then he will execute the THEN clause of the IF by moving forward and turning to his left. The program fragment on the right will first move Karel forward to the next corner and then will instruct him to test for a beeper. Since this corner does not contain a beeper, Karel will execute the ELSE clause of the IF, which causes him to turn to his right. Thus, top factoring in this example does not preserve execution equivalence.

Why can we correctly use top factoring in the first example but not in the second? Our first instruction can be top factored safely because the test that determines which way Karel is facing is not changed by having him move forward. Therefore, whether he moves first or not, the test will remain the same. But in the second example, the move changes the corner on which Karel checks for a beeper, so he is not really checking the same test. The general rule is that we may top factor an instruction only when the test that Karel performs does not change between the original and factored version of the instruction.

The fourth and final transformation is used to remove redundant tests in nested IF instructions. We call this transformation <u>redundant-test factoring</u> and show one application of this rule.

```
IF facing-west                    IF facing-west
  THEN                              THEN
     BEGIN                            BEGIN
       move;                            move;
       IF facing-west                   turnleft
          THEN turnleft             END
     END
```

In the instruction on the left, there is no need for the nested IF instruction to recheck the condition facing-west. The THEN clause of the outside IF is only executed if Karel is facing west, and the move inside this THEN clause does not change the direction that Karel is facing; therefore, facing-west is always true when Karel executes the nested IF instruction. This argument shows that Karel always executes the THEN clause of the nested IF. So, the entire nested IF instruction can be replaced by turnleft, as has been done in the instruction on the right. Once again, this transformation preserves execution equivalence. A similar transformation applies whenever we look for a redundant test in an ELSE clause, though in an ELSE clause we know <test> to be false.

This transformation is also a bit more subtle than bottom factoring, and we must be careful when trying to use it. The potential difficulty is that intervening instructions might change Karel's position in an unknown way. For example, if instead of the move instruction we had written a turnaround-only-if-blocked instruction, we could not have used redundant-test factoring. In this case we cannot be sure whether Karel would be facing west or east when he had to execute the nested IF.

These four transformations can help us make our programs smaller, simpler, more logical, and—most important—more readable.

4.7 The Dangling ELSE

This section examines a syntactic anomaly of nested IF instructions. Look at the following two nested IFs, and carefully study how each is boxed. We have kept the bracketed words in these instructions, because their exact replacements do not affect our discussion.

```
IF  <test-1>                      IF  <test-1>
  THEN                              THEN
     IF  <test-2>                      IF  <test-2>
       THEN  <instruction-1>             THEN  <instruction-1>
       ELSE  <instruction-2>         ELSE  <instruction-2>
```

The difference between these two instructions is the boxing of the ELSE clause. In the first instruction, the ELSE is boxed with the nested IF, but in the second the ELSE is boxed with the outside IF. These are obviously two different instructions, yet Karel cannot tell them apart. To prove this to yourself, ignore the boxing and read each of the instructions. Both contain exactly the same words in exactly the same order.

We are therefore faced with two questions: First, if we read this instruction to Karel, which way would he box it? Second, if we want Karel to box the instruction the other way, how would we tell him to do so? This anomaly is known in programming jargon as the dangling ELSE problem.

The first question is answered by introducing a new grammar rule. This rule states that whenever Karel is read an ELSE clause, he boxes it with the most recently read IF instruction that it can be a part of. Therefore, if we read Karel the preceding instruction, he boxes it like the previous boxing on the left.

We next show two related solutions to the second question. Each of the following two instructions is interpreted by Karel in a manner similar to the previous boxing on the right.

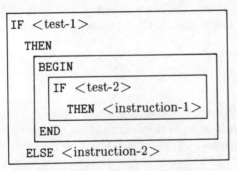

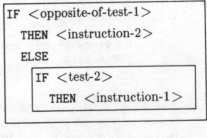

In the example on the left, we use a BEGIN/END block to inform Karel that the nested IF instruction is of the IF/THEN type. When Karel boxes this block, the END reserved word forces him to conclude that he has seen the entire nested IF instruction. He must treat the BEGIN/END block as a single instruction, and he must completely box all instructions within this block before reaching the END delimiter; thus, when the ELSE is finally read to Karel, there is only one IF instruction with which he can match it.

But we do not have to stop here. Now that we have the instruction on the left, we can simplify it by using test reversal. To perform test reversal, we replace <test-1> by its opposite and switch the THEN and ELSE clauses; now the BEGIN/END block in the ELSE clause is unnecessary, so it can be removed. These two steps result in the instruction on the right, which allows Karel to match the ELSE with the outside IF unambiguously.

4.8 Problem Set

The problems in this section require the use of the IF instruction in its two forms. Try using stepwise refinement on these problems, but no matter what method you use to obtain a solution, write a clear and understandable program. Keep the nesting level small for those problems requiring nested IF instructions. Use proper punctuation and grammar, especially within the THEN and ELSE clauses of the IF instructions. Carefully simulate each definition and program that you write to ensure that there are no execution or intent errors.

▶1. Define face-south, a new instruction that executes by facing Karel south regardless of the direction he is initially facing. First, do this without using face-north as a known instruction. Experiment with different forms of the IF/THEN and IF/THEN/ELSE instructions. Next, write face-south assuming that the instruction face-north has already been defined. This second definition should be much simpler, and given that face-north is correct, it should be easy to convince anyone of the correctness of face-south.

2. Look at the following instruction. Is there a simpler, execution equivalent instruction? If so, write it down; if not, explain why not. **Hint:** A simplifying transformation for the IF may prove useful. Common sense helps too.

```
IF not-next-to-a-beeper
   THEN move
   ELSE move
```

3. Assume that Karel is on a corner with either one or two beepers. Write a new instruction that commands him to face north if he is started on a corner with one beeper and to face south if he is started on a corner with two beepers. Besides facing him in the required direction, after Karel has executed this instruction there must be no beepers left on his corner. Name this instruction find-next-direction.

4. Write another version of find-next-direction (see the previous problem). In this version, Karel must eventually face the same directions, but he also must leave the same number of beepers on the corner as were there originally.

5. Write an instruction that turns Karel off if he is completely surrounded by walls, unable to move in any direction. If he is not completely surrounded, Karel should execute this instruction by leaving himself turned on, and by remaining on the same corner, facing the same direction in which he started. Name this instruction turnoff-if-surrounded. **Hint:** To write this instruction correctly, you will need to include a turnoff inside it. This combination is perfectly legal, but it is the first time that you will have to use a turnoff instruction outside of the BEGINNING-OF-EXECUTION/END-OF-EXECUTION block.

▶6. Program Karel to run a mile long steeplechase. The steeplechase course is similar to the hurdle race, but here the barriers can be one, two, or three blocks high. Figure 4–4 shows one sample initial situation, where Karel's final situation and path are indicated on the right.

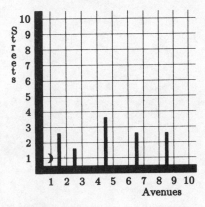

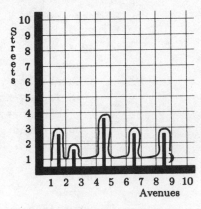

Initial Situation   Final Situation and Karel's Path

Figure 4–4: A Steeplechase Race Task

▶7. Rewrite and box the following instruction, taking care to interpret all of Karel's grammar rules correctly. This instruction uses nested IFs to face Karel toward the east; verify that it is correct by simulation. **Hint:** When trying to box this instruction, put yourself in Karel's place and ignore the instruction's indentation. One way of doing this is to have someone read you the instruction. While they are reading the instruction, you should box it—after all, this is exactly what Karel does.

```
DEFINE-NEW-INSTRUCTION face-east AS
BEGIN
  IF not-facing-east
    THEN
        IF facing-west
          THEN
              BEGIN
                 turnleft;
                 turnleft
              END
      ELSE
          IF facing-north
            THEN turnright
            ELSE turnleft
  END
```

8. The current version of **mystery-instruction** is syntactically correct, but very difficult to read. Simplify it by using the **IF** transformations.

```
DEFINE-NEW-INSTRUCTION mystery-instruction AS
BEGIN
  IF facing-west
    THEN
      BEGIN
        move;
        turnright;
        IF facing-north
          THEN move;
        turnaround ( f - south)
      END
    ELSE
      BEGIN
        move;
        turnleft;
        move;
        turnaround
      END
END
```

▶9. Write an instruction named **follow-wall-right**, assuming that whenever Karel executes this instruction there is a wall directly to his right. Figure 4–5 shows all four of the different position changes that he must be able to make. This instruction is the cornerstone for a program that directs Karel to escape from a maze (this maze-escape problem is Problem 5.6–11).

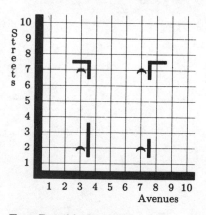

Four Possible Situations

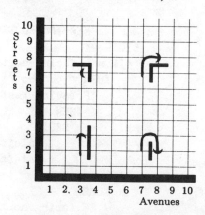

Their Respective Movements

Figure 4–5: The **follow-wall-right** Specification

CHAPTER FIVE

INSTRUCTIONS THAT REPEAT

This chapter completes our discussion of the instructions that are built into Karel's vocabulary. The two new instructions we shall learn are ITERATE and WHILE. Both of these instructions can repeatedly execute any instruction that Karel understands, including nested ITERATE and WHILE instructions. These additions greatly enhance the conciseness and power of the robot programming language. Also, in Section 5.5 we shall construct a complex, room-escaping robot program by using stepwise refinement and all of the instructions we have learned.

5.1 The ITERATE Instruction

When we program Karel, it is sometimes necessary to have him repeat an instruction a fixed number of times. We previously handled this problem by writing the instruction as many times as needed. The ITERATE instruction provides us with a shorthand notation that instructs Karel to repeat another instruction a specified number of times. It has the following general form.

```
ITERATE <positive-number> TIMES
    <instruction>
```

This instruction introduces the reserved words ITERATE and TIMES. The bracketed word <positive-number> tells Karel how many times to execute the instruction that replaces <instruction>. We refer to <instruction> as the body of the ITERATE instruction, and we shall also use the term ITERATE loop to suggest verbally that this instruction loops back and executes itself (no, it does not commit suicide). Our first example of an ITERATE loop is another definition of turnright.

```
DEFINE-NEW-INSTRUCTION turnright AS
BEGIN
    ITERATE 3 TIMES
        turnleft
END
```

As a second example, we rewrite the harvest-a-furrow instruction that was written in Section 3.8. This definition originally comprised nine primitive instructions, but by using ITERATE we can define this instruction more concisely.

With this new, more general version of `harvest-a-furrow`, we can also easily increase or decrease the number of beepers harvested per furrow; all we need to change is the number in the ITERATE instruction.

```
DEFINE-NEW-INSTRUCTION harvest-a-furrow AS
BEGIN
    pickbeeper;
    ITERATE 4 TIMES
      BEGIN
        move;
        pickbeeper
      END
END
```

Finally, we show an ITERATE instruction nested within another ITERATE instruction. Carefully observe the way that this instruction is boxed, for this is a strong clue to how Karel executes it.

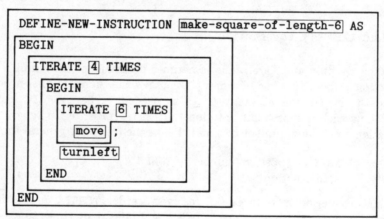

If we assume no blocking walls, this instruction moves Karel around the perimeter of a square whose sides are 6 blocks long. The outside ITERATE instruction loops a total of 4 times, once for each side of the square. Each time the outside ITERATE loop's body is executed, Karel executes two instructions. He first executes the nested ITERATE, which makes one side of the 6 block square. Then Karel executes the turnleft, which prepares him to trace the next side. Thus, Karel executes a total of 24 moves and 4 left turns, which are arranged in an order that makes him travel in a square.

5.2 The WHILE Instruction

In this section we explain the WHILE instruction and analyze many of its interesting properties. It is the most powerful instruction that is built into Karel's vocabulary.

5.2.1 Why WHILE is Needed

To motivate the need for a WHILE instruction, we look at what should be a simple programming task. Assume that Karel is initially facing east on some street, and somewhere east of him on that same street is a beeper. Karel's task is to move forward until he is on the same corner as the beeper, and then pick it up. Despite its simple description, this program is impossible to write with our current repertoire of instructions. Two attempts at solving this problem might be written as follows.

```
IF not-next-to-a-beeper          ITERATE ? TIMES
   THEN move;                        move;
IF not-next-to-a-beeper          pickbeeper
   THEN move;
        ⋮
IF not-next-to-a-beeper
   THEN move;
pickbeeper
```

We can interpret what is meant by these instructions, but Karel understands neither "…" nor "?". The difficulty is that we do not know in advance how many move instructions Karel must execute before he arrives at the same corner as the beeper; we do not even have a guaranteed upper limit. The beeper may be on Karel's starting street corner, or it may be a million blocks away. Karel must be able to accomplish this task without knowing in advance the number of corners that he will pass before reaching the beeper. We must program Karel to execute move instructions repeatedly, until he senses that he is next to the beeper. What we need is an instruction that combines the repetition ability of the ITERATE instruction with the testing ability of the IF instruction.

5.2.2 The WHILE Instruction

The WHILE instruction commands Karel to repeat another instruction as long as some test remains true. It is executed somewhat similarly to an IF/THEN instruction, except that the WHILE instruction repeatedly executes itself as long as <test> is true. The general form of the WHILE instruction is given below.

```
WHILE <test> DO
   <instruction>
```

The new reserved word WHILE starts this instruction, and the word DO separates <test> from the body of the WHILE loop. The vocabulary words that can replace <test> are the same ones that are used in the IF instructions.

Karel executes a WHILE loop by first checking <test> in his current situation. If <test> is true, Karel executes <instruction> and then re-executes the entire WHILE loop; if <test> is false, Karel is finished with the WHILE instruction, and he continues by executing the instructions following the entire WHILE loop. Here is a sample WHILE instruction, which solves the problem that motivated this discussion.

```
DEFINE-NEW-INSTRUCTION go-to-beeper AS
BEGIN
  WHILE not-next-to-a-beeper DO
    move
END
```

This instruction moves Karel forward as long as not-next-to-a-beeper is true. When Karel is finally next to a beeper, he finishes executing the WHILE loop. The following instruction is another simple example of a WHILE loop, and we shall examine its behavior in detail.

```
DEFINE-NEW-INSTRUCTION clear-corner-of-beepers AS
BEGIN
  WHILE next-to-a-beeper DO
    pickbeeper
END
```

This instruction commands Karel to pick up all of the beepers on a corner. Let's simulate Karel's execution of this instruction on a corner containing two beepers. He first determines whether next-to-a-beeper is true or false. Finding it true, he executes the body of the WHILE, which is the pickbeeper instruction. Then he re-executes the entire WHILE loop. Karel again finds that he is next to a beeper (one is still left), so he again executes the body of the WHILE loop. After picking up the second beeper, Karel re-executes the entire WHILE instruction—although we know that there are no beepers remaining, Karel is unaware of this fact until he rechecks the WHILE loop test. Now he rechecks the test and discovers that next-to-a-beeper is false, so he finishes executing the WHILE loop. Because the entire definition consists of one WHILE loop, he is finished executing clear-corner-of-beepers. It appears that no matter how many beepers are initially on the corner, Karel will eventually pick them all up when he executes this instruction.

But what happens if Karel executes clear-corner-of-beepers on a corner that has no beepers? In this special case, <test> is false the first time that the WHILE instruction is executed, so the WHILE body is not executed at all. Therefore, Karel also handles this situation correctly. The key fact to remember about a WHILE instruction is that until Karel discovers that <test> has become false—and it may be false the first time—Karel repeatedly checks <test> and executes the loop's body.

5.2.3 Infinite WHILE Loops

What happens if Karel executes the following curious WHILE loop? Observe that the body of this WHILE loop is a turnleft instruction; the body of this loop is not a pickbeeper.

```
DEFINE-NEW-INSTRUCTION incorrect-clear-corner-of-beepers AS
BEGIN
    WHILE next-to-a-beeper DO
        turnleft
END
```

First, let's assume that there are no beepers on the corner. In this case next-to-a-beeper is false, so Karel immediately finishes executing the WHILE instruction. This situation is handled correctly, but what happens if there is at least one beeper on the corner? In this case next-to-a-beeper is true, so Karel executes the turnleft in the body of the loop and re-executes the entire WHILE instruction. Do you see the impending problem? He rechecks the test, finds that he is still next to a beeper, turns left again, and re-executes the WHILE instruction. Karel will continue executing this WHILE instruction forever, spinning like a top.

This problem is known as getting Karel stuck in an infinite loop. Infinite looping is a kind of intent error, because Karel cannot determine when he is in an infinite loop. This possibility is the price that we must pay for allowing Karel the ability to execute an instruction an unknown number of times. The WHILE is the only instruction that can cause Karel to get stuck in an infinite loop; the only other repetitive instruction is ITERATE, which always finishes since we specify in the instruction itself how many times it will loop. We add infinite loops to our list of pitfalls to avoid, so we should carefully check each WHILE loop that we write to verify that it eventually terminates.

5.2.4 A Formal Property of the WHILE Instruction

So far, in this chapter we have discussed three definitions containing WHILE loops. The first WHILE loop tested not-next-to-a-beeper; when Karel finished executing this loop, he was next to a beeper. The next WHILE loop tested next-to-a-beeper; when Karel finished executing this loop, he was not next to any beepers. The third WHILE loop never terminated.

An important formal property of the WHILE instruction is that when it finishes executing, <test> is known to be false. This is proven by paraphrasing the execution rule for WHILE loops: "if <test> is true, then the loop continues executing." Therefore, if a WHILE loop finishes executing—and we have seen that not all of them do—<test> is guaranteed to be false. We can use this property to write instructions that are required to make a certain condition true. Whenever we must make <test> true, we write something similar to the following WHILE instruction into our program.

    WHILE <opposite-of-test> DO
        <instruction>

This general form is possible because Karel's vocabulary includes both the positive and negative forms of each test. For example, if we want next-to-a-beeper to be true, we write a WHILE loop with <opposite-of-test> replaced by not-next-to-a-beeper. If we want front-is-blocked to be true, we write a WHILE loop with <opposite-of-test> replaced by front-is-clear. Whenever a WHILE loop terminates, the <opposite-of-test> is guaranteed to be false, which means that <test> is guaranteed to be true.

How do we ensure that a WHILE loop always terminates? We should write the loop body with the following thought: Each time the loop body executes, Karel should perform some action that brings him closer to finishing the loop. An infinite loop occurs whenever <instruction> does not cause Karel to progress toward making <test> false. In the incorrect-clear-corner-of-beepers instruction, for example, it is obvious that Karel's execution of turnleft does not bring him any closer to having picked up all the beepers. Unfortunately, infinite loops are not always so easy to spot in more complex instructions.

To demonstrate one more WHILE instruction, we show a second, elegant way to define the face-north instruction.

    DEFINE-NEW-INSTRUCTION face-north AS
    BEGIN
        WHILE not-facing-north DO
            turnleft
    END

When this instruction finishes executing, <test> will be false according to the formal WHILE property. In this example, not-facing-north will become false—or by removing the double negative, facing-north will be true. But we have shown only that this instruction is partially correct. We must also prove that by continually executing turnleft instructions, the WHILE loop will eventually terminate. Because each turnleft changes the direction that Karel faces by 90°, we can guarantee that he will be facing north after at most three left turns. This same argument allowed us to conclude in Section 4.3.3 that our first definition of the face-north instruction is correct.

5.2.5 Verifying WHILE Loops

We pause here for a minute and reflect on how we can verify programs that use WHILE loops. It was bad enough when we found in Section 4.5 that small programs with IF instructions sometimes need to execute correctly in trillions of different initial situations. Now we have introduced an instruction that must be capable of working correctly in an unbounded number of initial situations.

How can we possibly verify programs that use this type of instruction? In general, there is no useful, rigorous way to verify robot programs that use WHILE loops; instead, we settle for probable correctness based on the following argument. (We faced a similar problem and chose a similar solution when verifying complex programs that used IF instructions.)

To argue that a WHILE instruction is correct, we rely on the following informal method of reasoning.

- First, we must show that the instruction works correctly in a situation where <test> is false.

- Second, we must show that each time the loop body is executed, Karel's new situation (after executing the body) is a *simpler* and *similar* version of his old situation (before executing the body). By *simpler*, we mean that Karel now has less work to do before finishing the loop, and by *similar* we mean that Karel's situation has not changed radically during his execution of the loop body.

- From these two facts we can conclude that no matter how many times the loop body must be executed, the instruction performs correctly. We can also conclude that the WHILE instruction eventually terminates, because each time Karel executes the loop body he is performing some action that brings him closer to having <test> become false.

As an example, let's argue that the clear-corner-of-beepers instruction is correct by using this style of reasoning. First, if there are no beepers on Karel's corner in the initial situation, the WHILE instruction performs correctly by immediately finishing. Second, if there are any beepers on the corner before the loop body executes, there will be one less beeper there after the loop body executes. This is the desired simpler (one less beeper) and similar (Karel is still on the same corner ready to pick up beepers) situation.[1] Karel will continue executing the loop body and removing beepers from the corner until no beepers remain. He then correctly finishes executing the loop in this no-beeper situation, as shown in the first step of this argument. Thus, we have argued that clear-corner-of-beepers is correct.

Generally, even this style of reasoning is too difficult to apply to complicated WHILE instructions. Therefore, few complex robot programs are actually argued

---

[1]Consider what would happen if, instead of instructing Karel to pick up a beeper, the body of the WHILE loop caused him to move to another corner. Karel's new situation may be simpler— the new corner may contain no beepers at all—but Karel cannot correctly finish his task because this situation is too unlike his original situation: Karel is no longer on the same corner.

correct by this method. Instead, instructions are tested in many different initial situations. For the clear-corner-of-beepers instruction, a typical testing argument might be, "I simulated Karel's execution in initial situations with 0, 1, 2, 3, and 7 beepers on the corner, and in each case the instruction worked correctly. Because all other situations are similar to these, the instruction probably works correctly in all situations." (Can you write a clear-corner-of-beepers definition that works correctly in these situations but fails in others? It can be done; see Problem 5.6–12 for details.)

We hope that the test situations we use typify all possible situations that Karel may encounter, but being human, we are limited in our ability to discover obscure situations. Although arguments based on testing give us a certain measure of confidence that our WHILE instructions are correct, it is not the same thing as verifying them. The verifying versus testing dilemma can be boiled down to the aphorism: "Testing only shows the presence of bugs, not their absence."

Since we must test the instructions that we write, we should be aware of a rule of thumb that is useful for hand-simulating WHILE loops. Because the beginning and end of a loop's execution are prone toward errors, each WHILE loop should be closely observed during its first few and last few repetitions. We should also carefully simulate a few repetitions in the middle of the loop, just to ensure that it is correct too.

5.2.6 When the <test> of a WHILE is Checked

The rules in Section 5.2.2 that explained how Karel executes a WHILE instruction are correct, yet unless read carefully, they may leave room for some ambiguity. In this section we closely examine the execution rules for a WHILE instruction and point out a common misconception about when Karel checks <test>. Let's simulate the following instruction cautiously.

```
DEFINE-NEW-INSTRUCTION harvest-line AS
BEGIN
    WHILE next-to-a-beeper DO
        BEGIN
            pickbeeper;
            move
        END
END
```

This instruction correctly commands Karel to pick up a line of beepers. He finishes executing this instruction after moving one block beyond the final corner that has a beeper. Of course, a gap in the line would also cause Karel to believe that he is at the end of the beeper line.

This instruction's definition contains the first WHILE loop body we have seen that is a sequence of instructions; consequently, the loop body must be contained in a BEGIN/END block. First, let's correctly simulate this instruction in detail for a line of two beepers. Karel starts his task on the same corner as the first beeper. He executes the WHILE instruction and finds that the test is true, so he next executes the body of the loop. The loop body instructs him to pick up the beeper and then move to the next corner. Now he re-executes the loop; the test is checked again, and Karel again senses that he is next to a beeper. Therefore, Karel picks up the second beeper and moves forward. He then executes the loop again. Now when he checks the test, he finds that his corner is beeperless, so he is finished executing the WHILE loop. The definition of harvest-line contains only one instruction—this WHILE loop—so harvest-line is also finished.

The point demonstrated here is that Karel checks <test> only before he executes the body of the loop. He is totally insensitive to the <test> while executing instructions inside the loop body. To state this another way, once Karel starts executing the loop body, he does not recheck <test> until he starts to re-execute the entire WHILE instruction, which happens only after he has completely executed the loop body.

A common misconception among novice programmers is that Karel checks <test> after each instruction he executes inside the loop body. It is easy to arrive at this misconception when dealing with a WHILE loop that contains only one instruction in its body, for in this case the two rules yield identical results. But in multiple instruction loop bodies, like the one in harvest-line, there is a distinguishable difference between these two rules.

Let's see what would happen if Karel used the incorrect rule to execute the harvest-line instruction in the two-beeper situation. This rule would force Karel to finish the WHILE loop as soon as he was not next to a beeper. Karel would start by testing whether he was next to a beeper. Finding the test true, he would execute the loop body. This is fine so far, but after executing the first instruction in the loop body, the pickbeeper, Karel would not be next to a beeper anymore—he has just put the one that he was next to into his beeper-bag. So, according to this second, incorrect execution rule, Karel would now be finished with the loop. This rule would limit Karel to picking up only one beeper, regardless of the length of the beeper line.

We emphasize that the first of these rules is the one that Karel uses; the second is incorrect.

5.3 Repeating Instructions and Block Structure

This section examines what can happen to a repeating instruction when a necessary BEGIN/END block is omitted. We discuss a WHILE instruction in our example, but the same type of argument holds for the ITERATE instruction as well. Karel's task in this section is again to harvest a line of beepers, except this time the end of the line is marked by a wall. We can assume that every corner between Karel's starting corner and the wall contains exactly one beeper. One of the many possible initial situations for this task is given in Figure 5–1.

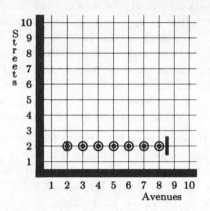

Figure 5–1: A Line-Harvesting Task

The following instruction correctly accomplishes the task.

```
DEFINE-NEW-INSTRUCTION harvest-to-wall AS
BEGIN
    pickbeeper;
    WHILE front-is-clear DO
      BEGIN
        move;
        pickbeeper
      END
END
```

Notice that without the first **pickbeeper**, Karel would **move** first, before picking up the beeper on his starting corner. If you think the situation can be remedied by removing the first **pickbeeper** and then switching the instructions in the body of the WHILE loop, think again. Although Karel would now pick up the first beeper, this instruction would leave the last beeper unharvested.

Generally, observe that the number of beepers that Karel must pick up is one greater than the number of moves that he must perform (in Figure 5–1, he must pick up seven beepers, but move only six times). Simple counting arguments such as this one can frequently help you determine which instructions must be inside of a loop and which instructions must be outside of a loop. It would be correct to remove the first **pickbeeper** and switch the two instructions in the loop body if we added an extra **pickbeeper** at the end of this definition, directly after the WHILE loop. But we prefer writing this special case first, to make it more visible.

What would Karel do if we read him the previous instruction without the **BEGIN** and **END** delimiters that surround the loop body? Karel would box and interpret the instruction as follows.

```
DEFINE-NEW-INSTRUCTION incorrect-harvest-to-wall AS
BEGIN
    pickbeeper ;
    WHILE front-is-clear DO
        move ;
    pickbeeper
END
```

Box harvest-to-wall and then compare these two instructions. Both are syntactically correct, but notice that the boxing is different. The correct definition consists of two instructions: the pickbeeper and a WHILE loop whose body contains a sequence of two instructions. The incorrect definition consists of three instructions: the pickbeeper, the WHILE loop containing only the move within its body, and the final pickbeeper instruction. The results of Karel's execution of each of these instructions are shown in Figure 5–2.

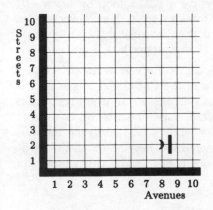
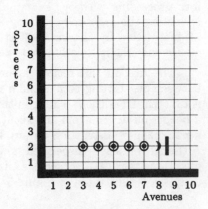

harvest-to-wall   Intent Error in incorrect-harvest-to-wall

Figure 5–2: Karel's Execution of Both Instructions

Karel executes the incorrect instruction by first picking up the beeper on his starting corner. The WHILE loop then moves Karel forward until his front becomes blocked, without commanding him to pick up any additional beepers. This happens because the faulty loop body contains only the move instruction. When Karel's front is finally blocked, he exits the WHILE loop and then executes the second pickbeeper instruction. The result of executing incorrect-harvest-to-wall is that Karel picks up only the first and last beepers in the line.

Can you think of an initial situation in which this incorrect instruction causes an error shutoff? How about an initial situation in which this instruction actually performs correctly? Both situations do exist. Here again we have an instruction that executes correctly in some situations and incorrectly in others; it sometimes causes an execution error and sometimes results in an intent error.

This discussion—the last of its kind—is similar to our previous boxing-error discussions. The central idea in all of the omitted-BEGIN/END-block errors is that we must be aware of exactly how Karel boxes and executes our programs. Incorrect use of BEGIN/END blocks is such a common error for novices, I wanted to show in detail, for each kind of instruction, what happens when such a mistake is made. Sometimes Karel recognizes the mistake as a syntactic error, but most of the time a subtle intent error results; consequently, we should check our programs carefully for missing BEGIN/END blocks.

5.4 IF Instructions in WHILE Loops

Before starting the big programming example in this chapter, we shall uncover another frequent cause of trouble and misunderstanding when we simulate Karel's programs. This problem involves IF instructions that are inside the body of a WHILE loop. Confusion might arise because both IFs and WHILEs perform tests and have similar execution rules. We summarize each execution rule before proceeding with our example. Karel executes a WHILE loop by repeatedly executing the loop body as long as <test> remains true. Karel executes an IF instruction by checking <test> once, and then executing the appropriate clause once (he is then finished executing the IF instruction).

The task in this section again requires Karel to harvest a line of beepers between his starting corner and a wall that marks the end of the beeper line. It is different from the last task in that we do not guarantee that every corner has a beeper on it. To avoid an execution error, Karel must not attempt to execute a pickbeeper instruction on any barren corner while he is harvesting the line. Although we leave unspecified how many corners have beepers on them, we do guarantee that each corner has either zero or one beeper on it. One example of this task is illustrated in Figure 5–3.

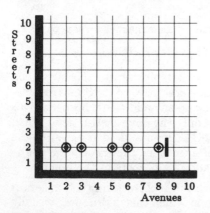

One Initial Situation

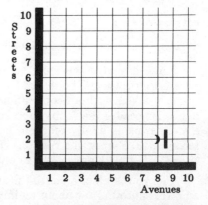

The Final Situation

Figure 5–3: A Sparse Line-Harvesting Task

The following instruction is a slight modification of the original harvest-to-wall instruction. As before, the purpose of the WHILE loop is to move Karel ahead until he reaches the wall. But in this definition, Karel uses the IF instruction in the body of the loop to decide whether he should execute a pickbeeper. He makes this decision once for each corner.

```
DEFINE-NEW-INSTRUCTION sparse-harvest-to-wall AS
BEGIN
  IF next-to-a-beeper
    THEN pickbeeper;
  WHILE front-is-clear DO
    BEGIN
      move;
      IF next-to-a-beeper
        THEN pickbeeper
    END
END
```

The execution of this definition in the initial situation of Figure 5–3 starts by having Karel execute the first IF instruction, which results in his picking up the first beeper. He then executes the second instruction in the definition—the WHILE loop. Karel finds that his front is clear, so he moves ahead and then executes the IF instruction, checking for a beeper on his new corner. Because he is next to a beeper, he executes the pickbeeper in the THEN clause. Karel has now completely executed the loop body, and therefore he re-executes the WHILE loop. Once again he checks whether his front is clear. It is, so he executes the loop body by both moving ahead to the corner of 2nd St. and 4th Ave. and then executing the IF instruction. On this corner Karel is not next to a beeper, so he does not execute the pickbeeper in the THEN clause. Again he is finished with the IF instruction and the loop body, so he re-executes the WHILE loop.

Let's assume that Karel keeps up the good work and soon finds himself on 7th Avenue, about to re-execute the WHILE loop. His front is clear, so he moves forward and picks up the last beeper. Again he executes the WHILE loop, but this time finds that his front is now blocked, and thus finishes the instruction. Karel has correctly accomplished his task in this initial situation.

If we wanted to simplify sparse-harvest-to-wall, we could do so by replacing each IF/THEN instruction by the defined pickbeeper-if-present instruction. Not only would this substitution decrease the size of the definition, it would decrease the level of instruction nesting as well; the result would be a more readable instruction.

Can we easily modify this instruction to handle situations that have more than one beeper per corner? Yes, we can use clear-corner-of-beepers and write the following instruction.

```
DEFINE-NEW-INSTRUCTION many-beeper-sparse-harvest-to-wall AS
BEGIN
  clear-corner-of-beepers;
  WHILE front-is-clear DO
    BEGIN
      move;
      clear-corner-of-beepers
    END
END
```

We have now written four instructions that harvest lines of beepers. Each instruction was slightly more general then the previous one, and each was written by modifying an already written instruction. Sometimes it is too hard for us to immediately write a program that solves Karel's required task; there are too many details to keep in mind at one time. If we are unable to make any progress by using stepwise refinement, a good rule of thumb is to try solving a similar but simpler task. If the simpler task is similar enough to the original, it will be easy for us to modify the simple solution to solve the original task. Of course, finding the right "similar but simpler" task is frequently difficult. It is not easy to decide how to simplify the task—to determine which details should be ignored because we can modify our program to account for them later. The more programming experience we acquire, the easier it is for us to decide correctly.

In general, we should always strive to re-use our previous work. Many programs are slight variations of previously written programs, or are similar enough to allow copying large portions of already written and tested instructions. We should accumulate a library of useful instructions and programs, which we can consult whenever we must write a new program.

5.4.1 A Syntax Error

Here is a syntax error that may be difficult to spot. Can you quickly determine what is syntactically wrong with the following instruction?

```
IF next-to-a-beeper
  DO pickbeeper
```

Either you do see the error or you do not; studying the instruction will probably do you no good. The error is that the reserved word DO does not belong before the THEN clause; the word THEN belongs there, of course. But this instruction reads so naturally that it is hard for our mind to interject, "Hey, wait a minute, that's not legal here." This is another example of an error that is hard for the human mind to discover, but is trivial for Karel's small-but-precise intellect to spot.

Often, programming errors are hard to find, but once discovered they are painfully obvious. Do not be too upset with yourself when you find these errors.

If you find a "stupid" error, do not think "I'm really dumb"; instead, think "I must be a genius to locate such an obscure and hard-to-spot error!" Granted, both are overstatements, but the second is closer to the truth than the first.

5.5 A Large Program Written by Stepwise Refinement

In this section we shall write a complex program by using stepwise refinement. The program instructs Karel to escape from any rectangular room that has an open doorway exactly one block wide. After escaping from the room, the program commands Karel to turn himself off.

Instead of deftly avoiding mistakes and presenting a polished program, we shall develop the program in a logical manner, commit the mistakes, recognize that mistakes have been made, and rewrite the program until it correctly performs the task. We proceed in this way because it more accurately reflects how complicated programs are written. We should be aware that throughout the development of a complex program, we are increasing our knowledge of the task. During this time we should constantly be on guard for errors in the program or discrepancies between the program and the specification of the task.

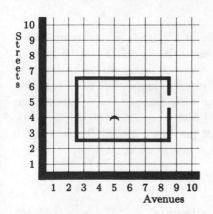
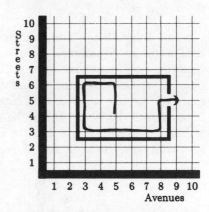

Initial Situation   Final Situation and Karel's Path

Figure 5–4: A Room-Escape Task

Figure 5–4 illustrates one possible initial situation for this task. We use this situation to create a general plan for escaping from rooms. Karel is initially somewhere in the room, facing some arbitrary direction. He starts the task by moving to the wall that he is initially facing. Karel then follows the inside perimeter of the room in a counter-clockwise direction, keeping his right side to the wall, until he senses the door on his right. He next exits through the door and finally turns himself off. Translating this informally stated escape plan, we obtain the following program.

```
BEGINNING-OF-EXECUTION
   go-to-wall;
   turnleft;
   follow-until-door-is-on-right;
   exit-door;
   turnoff
END-OF-EXECUTION
```

This program accomplishes the task, but in order to have Karel understand it, we must first define the instructions go-to-wall, follow-until-door-is-on-right, and exit-door. We begin by writing the go-to-wall instruction. This instruction must move Karel forward until he senses a wall directly in front of him. The test we eventually want to become true is front-is-blocked, so by using the formal WHILE property, we should be able to write this instruction as follows.

```
DEFINE-NEW-INSTRUCTION go-to-wall AS
BEGIN
   WHILE front-is-clear DO
      move
END
```

But although this simple instruction works in Figure 5–4, and many other similar initial situations, it does not work correctly in all initial situations. Unfortunately, there are some initial situations in which the WHILE instruction never terminates, leaving Karel stuck in an infinite loop. What is common among these situations is that Karel starts the task already facing toward the door, instead of toward one of the walls. When Karel executes this go-to-wall instruction in such a situation, he zooms out of the room without knowing that he has exited. One situation of this type is illustrated in Figure 5–5.

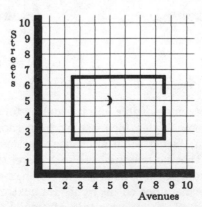

Figure 5–5: A Beyond-The-Horizon Situation for the Room-Escape Task

We call this type of situation a beyond-the-horizon situation. Normally, we write a program guided by a few initial situations that seem to cover all interesting aspects of the task. Although we would like to prove that all other situations are not too different from these sample situations, frequently the best we can do is hope. As we explore the problem and learn more about the task, we may discover situations that are beyond our original horizons—situations that are legal, but special trouble-causing cases. Once we have discovered a beyond-the-horizon situation, we should immediately simulate Karel's execution in it. If our suspicions are confirmed, and Karel does not perform as we intended, we must modify our program accordingly.

Let's construct a simple numerical argument that calculates the probability of finding a beyond-the-horizon situation by randomly testing Karel in legal initial situations. We restrict the following discussion to the room pictured in Figure 5–5. If we include all possible room sizes and door locations, the problems we encounter would become more severe.

In our example room, there are 24 possible corners on which Karel can start this task. Moreover, there are four ways that Karel can be placed on each corner (the four directions that he can face). Consequently, there are 96 different initial situations in which Karel can start this task. Out of this possible 96, there are only 6 placements of Karel that cause trouble for the go-to-wall instruction—Karel facing east on any one of the 6 corners on 5th Street. Thus, Karel malfunctions in less than 7% of all his possible starting positions. This argument demonstrates that randomly testing Karel in different initial situations is most likely to be ineffective. We must use our intellect to try to uncover those few situations where Karel's program may malfunction.

We must think hard to discover these situations, because they are not in our intuitive field of view. But our time is profitably spent doing so, because looking for beyond-the-horizon situations can only benefit us: if we find situations that cause errors, we can correct our program to account for them; if we cannot find any situations that cause errors, we have made progress toward convincing ourselves that our program is correct. Good programmers become skilled at extending their horizons and finding dangerous situations that prevent a program from accomplishing its task.

Returning to Karel's task, what can we do to correct our program? The basic plan is still valid, but we must modify the go-to-wall instruction, making sure that Karel finds a wall before he accidentally exits the room. The fact that the door is only one block wide is the key to our next attempt at writing go-to-wall. Instead of moving Karel straight ahead, we shall program him to move forward in a sideways shuffling motion.

Karel starts by checking for a wall directly in front of himself; if he does not find one, he next checks for a wall in front of the corner on his right. If Karel finds walls in neither of these places, he returns to his original corner and then moves one block forward. He repeats this right-left shuffling motion until he finds a wall. In this way he is guaranteed not to pass through the unnoticed door, because the door is only one block wide. The path Karel takes in the beyond-the-horizon situation is displayed in Figure 5–6. This same type of path works correctly in Figure 5–4 too.

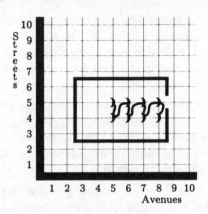

Figure 5–6: Karel's Shuffle Toward the Wall

So now let's rewrite `go-to-wall` to correspond to our new plan for moving Karel to a wall. We again use a WHILE loop with the same test, but in this instruction his forward motion is more complicated.

```
DEFINE-NEW-INSTRUCTION go-to-wall AS
BEGIN
  WHILE front-is-clear DO
    shuffle
END
```

We continue by using stepwise refinement to write `shuffle`.

```
DEFINE-NEW-INSTRUCTION shuffle AS
BEGIN
  sidestep-right;
  IF front-is-clear
    THEN
      BEGIN
        sidestep-back-left;
        move
      END
END
```

Finally, we write the simple sidestepping instructions directly in terms of Karel's primitive instructions and **turnright**.

```
DEFINE-NEW-INSTRUCTION sidestep-right AS
BEGIN
  turnright;
  move;
  turnleft
END
```

and

```
DEFINE-NEW-INSTRUCTION sidestep-back-left AS
BEGIN
  turnleft;
  move;
  turnright
END
```

Simulate these instructions in Figure 5–4 and Figure 5–6 to become better acquainted with this new **go-to-wall** instruction.

But even this plan has a small hidden wart on it; there are some initial situations in which Karel cannot perform a shuffle. For an example, look at the new beyond-the-horizon situation illustrated in Figure 5–7.

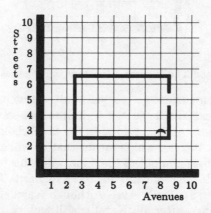

Figure 5–7: A Beyond-The-Horizon Situations that Prevents Shuffling

The wall on Karel's right prevents him from correctly performing the shuffle. Luckily, in situations like Figure 5–7, all we must do is turn Karel to the right; he will then be facing a wall, which easily satisfies the intent of **go-to-wall**. So, if Karel starts this task with his right side blocked by a wall, he merely turns to face this wall. Otherwise, his right is not blocked by a wall, and he can shuffle forward and to the right until his front becomes blocked. To accomplish this modification, we must rewrite only the definition of **go-to-wall**.

```
DEFINE-NEW-INSTRUCTION go-to-wall AS
BEGIN
  IF right-is-blocked
    THEN turnright
    ELSE
      WHILE front-is-clear DO
        shuffle
END
```

Well, as you may have suspected, there still is a problem with go-to-wall. This problem is illustrated in Figure 5-8, one of the beyondest-the-horizon situations you may ever see; it is the single situation in which the present go-to-wall instructions fails. This is the last difficulty we shall see before completing a correct version of go-to-wall, so please don't get disgusted and stop reading.

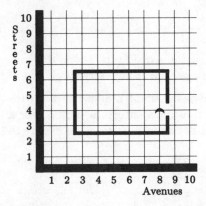

Figure 5–8: A Beyond-The-Horizon Situation that Causes an Error Shutoff

If Karel executes our current go-to-wall instruction in this initial situation, he will think that he can shuffle to the wall ahead—because his right is clear. So Karel starts executing the WHILE loop in the ELSE clause of go-to-wall. He first finds that his front is clear, which means that he will execute shuffle. The shuffle instruction moves him out of the door, where his front is still clear, then it moves him back inside the room and one block forward. This instruction leaves him facing north on 5th St. & 8th Ave. Although Karel's actions look strange, nothing is terribly wrong—after all, Karel is still looking in front of himself for a wall. He next rechecks front-is-clear in the WHILE loop and finds it true again, so he again starts to execute shuffle. But this time he is stopped by an error shutoff in sidestep-right, which commands him to turn right and then move—an impossibility in his current situation.

The problem is that we thought that Karel's right side could never become blocked if it was not originally blocked in his initial situation. Figure 5–8 showed us that this assumption is incorrect. We must modify go-to-wall so that Karel always checks to his right before executing a shuffle. This has been done in the following, finally correct definition of go-to-wall. Notice that the final definition consists of a WHILE loop that tests front-is-clear, so when this instruction finishes executing—and now we know that it always will—Karel's front is guaranteed to be blocked by one of the walls in the room.

```
DEFINE-NEW-INSTRUCTION go-to-wall AS
BEGIN
  WHILE front-is-clear DO
    IF right-is-blocked
      THEN turnright
      ELSE shuffle
END
```

The go-to-wall instruction now works correctly in any room. After executing go-to-wall, Karel will always have his front blocked by one of the four walls in the room. Because this instruction is so complicated and crucial to the task, you should immediately simulate Karel's execution of it in the initial situations illustrated in Figures 5-4 through 5-8. Do not proceed until you are familiar with exactly how Karel executes each instruction and what part each instruction plays in moving Karel to a wall.

Next we shall write the follow-until-door-is-on-right instruction. Recall that in the initial plan, Karel executes a turnleft instruction after go-to-wall; therefore, we can safely assume that just before Karel executes follow-until-door-is-on-right, his right is blocked by one wall of the room. This new instruction must satisfy two criteria.

- It must finish when Karel senses a door on his right-hand side. Karel senses this door when his right becomes clear.

- If a door has not been found, the instruction must keep Karel's right side adjacent to a wall while commanding him to follow the perimeter of the room in a counter-clockwise direction.

A condition that must always be true during the execution of an instruction is called an <u>invariant</u>. The invariant for the second criterion is that Karel's right-hand side must be adjacent to a wall (blocked) as he follows the perimeter of the room. To do this, Karel moves forward along a wall until he reaches a corner; when this happens, he turns to the left, ready to follow the next wall with his right side still blocked.

We begin by using the first criterion to write the instruction that finds the door. Karel must maneuver into a situation in which his right side is clear, so we again use the formal property of the WHILE instruction to write our definition.

```
DEFINE-NEW-INSTRUCTION follow-until-door-is-on-right AS
BEGIN
  WHILE right-is-blocked DO
    follow-perimeter
END
```

By the formal property of the WHILE instruction—again, provided that this loop terminates—Karel's right-hand side will be clear when Karel finishes executing follow-until-door-is-on-right. We now use the second criterion to write the follow-perimeter instruction.

```
DEFINE-NEW-INSTRUCTION follow-perimeter AS
BEGIN
  IF front-is-clear
     THEN move
     ELSE turnleft
END
```

This instruction moves Karel forward along a wall until he reaches a corner. Whenever he reaches a corner, Karel performs a left turn and is ready to continue following the perimeter with his right-hand side next to the new wall. The invariant that his right side is always next to a wall remains true, until he finally senses that the door is on his right-hand side.

Finally, we write the exit-door instruction. This is easy to do because it contains no complicated subparts. We can safely assume that Karel's right side is clear, since this instruction is executed directly after follow-until-door-is-on-right. The exit-door instruction can be written by using only Karel's primitive instructions and turnright.

```
DEFINE-NEW-INSTRUCTION exit-door AS
BEGIN
  turnright;
  move
END
```

We have now specified every instruction that Karel needs to accomplish his task. Although we cannot verify correctness, we should at least be able to verify that execution errors cannot occur. We can do this by showing that Karel never tries to execute a move instruction—the only primitive in this program capable of causing an error shutoff—when his front is blocked. I hope that this section has demonstrated how a difficult task can be programmed successfully by using the stepwise-refinement programming method. The entire program for this task is listed starting on page 84.

Before leaving this example, what would Karel do in the beyond-the-horizon situations illustrated in Figure 5–9? In both of these situations, he successfully escapes from the room and turns himself off, but not quite in the manner we may expect. Which instruction(s) must we change to remove the slight flaw from Karel's performance in the "unexpected door" situation? In this initial situation, Karel should exit the room and then turn himself off when he reaches the corner of 8th St. and 6th Ave.

Although I believe that this program is correct, there still may be other, undiscovered beyond-the-horizon situations that force it to fail. My mind is still open on the subject. This attitude is not false modesty; in earlier versions of this book, I incorrectly wrote the `go-to-wall` instruction by not discovering the beyond-the-horizon situation illustrated in Figure 5–8. Writing a completely, no doubts about it, 100% correct program, even for a seemingly simple task like this one, is a very difficult endeavor.

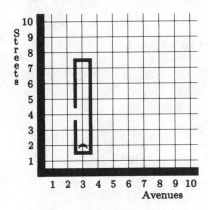

A Very Skinny Room

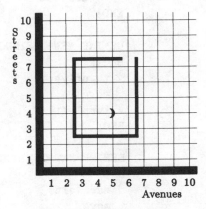

A Door in an Unexpected Place

Figure 5–9: Two Beyond-The-Horizon Situations

When attempting to write a large program, do not succumb to the "I've got to get it perfect the first time" syndrome. This leads to programmer's block: the inability to begin writing a program. You cannot foresee all of the difficulties that you will encounter while writing a program and, as already mentioned, it is impossible to try to plan an entire program in your head.

The most important step toward writing a program is putting something concrete down on paper. Once this is done, you can test the program by simulation, spot errors, and revise the program to remedy the errors. But with nothing written down, progress will be slow—and frustration will be high. Do not forget that a correct program is only half a solution; make sure that your program is also easily understandable.

Finally, if you revise your program to the point of losing the original thread of reasoning, you might want to rewrite the entire program. Rewriting a program is not as time consuming as you may think, because you can use all the knowledge that you gained while writing the previous version.

```
BEGINNING-OF-PROGRAM

  DEFINE-NEW-INSTRUCTION turnright AS
  BEGIN
    ITERATE 3 TIMES
      turnleft
  END;

  DEFINE-NEW-INSTRUCTION sidestep-right AS
  BEGIN
    turnright;
    move;
    turnleft
  END;

  DEFINE-NEW-INSTRUCTION sidestep-back-left AS
  BEGIN
    turnleft;
    move;
    turnright
  END;

  DEFINE-NEW-INSTRUCTION shuffle AS
  BEGIN
    sidestep-right;
    IF front-is-clear
      THEN
        BEGIN
          sidestep-back-left;
          move
        END
  END;

  DEFINE-NEW-INSTRUCTION go-to-wall AS
  BEGIN
    WHILE front-is-clear DO
      IF right-is-blocked
        THEN turnright
        ELSE shuffle
  END;
```

```
DEFINE-NEW-INSTRUCTION follow-perimeter AS
BEGIN
  IF front-is-clear
    THEN move
    ELSE turnleft
END;

DEFINE-NEW-INSTRUCTION follow-until-door-is-on-right AS
BEGIN
  WHILE right-is-blocked DO
    follow-perimeter
END;

DEFINE-NEW-INSTRUCTION exit-door AS
BEGIN
  turnright;
  move
END;


BEGINNING-OF-EXECUTION
  go-to-wall;
  turnleft;
  follow-until-door-is-on-right;
  exit-door;
  turnoff
END-OF-EXECUTION

END-OF-PROGRAM
```

5.6 Problem Set

The problems in this section require writing defini ions and programs that use WHILE instructions. Try using stepwise refinement and the formal WHILE property discussed in Section 5.2.4 when writing these definitions and programs. Test your solutions by simulating them in various initial situations, and try to find beyond-the-horizon situations too. Take care to write programs that avoid error shutoffs and infinite loops.

A common mistake among beginning programmers is trying to have each execution of a WHILE loop's body make too much progress. As a rule of thumb, try to have each execution of a WHILE loop's body make as little progress as possible (while still making some progress toward terminating the loop).

1. Write a new instruction for Karel named **empty-beeper-bag**. After Karel executes this instruction, his beeper-bag should be empty.

▶2. Write a new instruction called **go-to-origin** that positions Karel on 1st St. & 1st Ave. facing east, regardless of his initial location or the direction he is initially facing. Assume that there are no wall sections present. **Hint:** Use the south and west boundary walls as guides.

▶3. Study both of the following program fragments separately. What does each do? For each one, is there a simpler program fragment that is execution equivalent? If so, write it down; if not, explain why not. **Hint:** The formal WHILE property is useful.

```
WHILE not-next-to-a-beeper DO      WHILE not-next-to-a-beeper DO
  move;                              IF next-to-a-beeper
IF next-to-a-beeper                    THEN pickbeeper
  THEN pickbeeper                      ELSE move
  ELSE move
```

Describe the difference between the following two program fragments.

```
WHILE front-is-clear DO      IF front-is-clear
  move                         THEN move
```

4. Write an instruction that faces Karel east if he is on a corner with an even number of beepers, and faces him west if he is on a corner with an odd number of beepers (zero is considered an even number for this task). Karel can clear the corner of beepers while he is determining which direction to face. **Hint:** See Problem 4.8–3 for a more restricted version of this problem.

5. Program Karel to escape from a rectangular room if he can find a doorway. If there is no doorway, he must turn himself off. We cannot use the program written in Section 5.5 for this task, because executing this program in a

doorless room would cause Karel to run around inside the room forever; can you identify the instruction that will never finish executing? **Hint:** There is a slightly messy way to solve this problem without resorting to beepers. You can write the program this way, or you can assume that Karel has one beeper in his bag, which he can use to remember if he has circumnavigated the room. This program may require a separate turnoff instruction for the completely enclosed situation in addition to a turnoff instruction for the situation with a door.

6. Program Karel to run a super steeplechase. In this race the hurdles are arbitrarily high and the course has no fixed finish corner. The finish of each race course is marked by a beeper, which Karel must pick up before turning himself off. Figure 5–10 illustrates one possible course. Other courses may be longer and have higher hurdles.

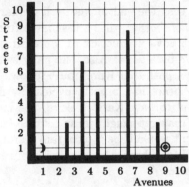

Figure 5–10: A Super Steeplechase

▶**7.** Program Karel to run a super-duper steeplechase. In this race the hurdles are arbitrarily high and arbitrarily wide. In each race course the finish is marked by a beeper, which Karel must pick up before turning himself off. Figure 5–11 illustrates one possible course.

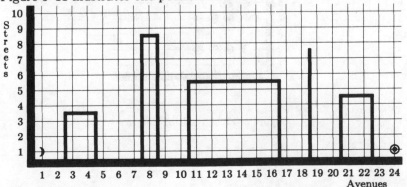

Figure 5–11: A Super-Duper Steeplechase

8. Write an instruction that harvests a rectangular field of any size. The field is guaranteed to be bordered by beeperless corners. Also, assume that every corner within the field has a beeper on it and that Karel starts out facing east on the lower left hand corner of the field.

▶9. Karel likes to take long meandering walks in the woods on his world, and even though he has a built-in compass, he sometimes cannot find his way back home. To alleviate this problem, before Karel walks in the woods he fills his beeper-bag and then he leaves a trail of beepers behind him (Karel obviously has not heard the story of Hansel and Gretel). Program Karel to follow this kind of path back home. There are many questions one can ask about this task. I shall try to clarify the specifications in the next paragraph.

Ignore the possibility that any wall boundaries or wall sections interfere with Karel, and assume that the end of his path is marked by two beepers on the same corner. Each beeper will be reachable from a previous beeper by the execution of one **move** instruction in some direction; there will be only one beeper reachable by a **move**. Also, the path will never cross over itself. See Figure 5–12 for a path that Karel must follow. **Hint:** Karel must probe each possible next corner in his path, eventually finding the correct one. It might prove useful to have Karel pick up the beepers as he follows the path; otherwise, he may get caught in an infinite loop going backward and forward. How difficult would it be to program Karel to follow the same type of path if we allowed for a beeper to be missing once in a while (but not two missing beepers in a row)?

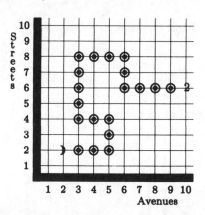

Figure 5–12: A Path of Beepers

10. Assume that Karel is somewhere in a completely enclosed rectangular room that contains one beeper. Program Karel to find the beeper, pick it up, and turn himself off.

11. Program Karel to escape from a maze that contains no islands. The exit of the maze is marked by placing a beeper on the first corner that is outside the maze, next to the right wall. This task can be accomplished by commanding Karel to move through the maze, with the invariant that his right side is always next to a wall. See Problem 4.8–9 for hints on the type of movements for which Karel must be programmed. Figure 5–13 shows one example of a maze.

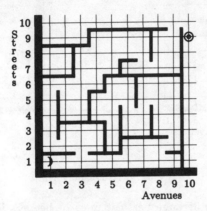

Figure 5–13: A Maze

There is a simpler way to program this task without using the instructions written in Problem 4.8–9. Try to write a shorter version of the maze-escaping program. **Hint:** Program Karel to make the minimal amount of progress toward his goal at each corner in the maze.

Finally, compare the maze escape problem with Problem 5.9–7, the Super-Duper Steeplechase. Do you see any similarities?

12. This problem is inspired by the discussion on the verification of WHILE loops (pages 66-68). Simulate Karel's execution of the following instruction in initial situations where he is on a corner with 0, 1, 2, 3, and 7 beepers.

```
DEFINE-NEW-INSTRUCTION will-this-clear-corner-of-beepers AS
BEGIN
    ITERATE 10 TIMES
        IF next-to-a-beeper
            THEN pickbeeper
END
```

State in exactly which initial situations this instruction works correctly. What happens in the other situations?

13. Program Karel to go on a treasure hunt. The treasure is marked by a corner containing 5 beepers. Other corners (including the corner on which Karel starts) contain clues, with each clue indicating in which direction Karel should next proceed. The clues are as follows: 1 beeper means Karel should next go north, 2 means west, 3 means south, and 4 means east. Karel should follow the clues until he reaches the treasure corner, where he should turn himself off. Figure 5–14 shows one possible treasure hunt.

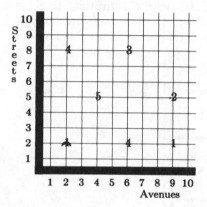

One Initial Situation

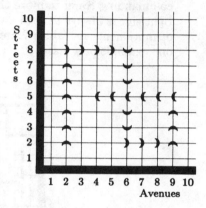

The Final Situation and Karel's Path

Figure 5–14: A Treasure Hunt

14. Program Karel to arrange vertical piles of beepers into ascending order. Each avenue, starting at the origin, will contain a vertical pile of one or more beepers. The first empty avenue will mark the end of the piles that need to be sorted. Figure 5–15 illustrates one of the many possible initial and final situations. (How difficult would it be to modify your program to arrange the piles of beepers into descending order?)

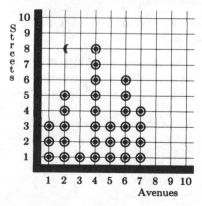

One Initial Situation

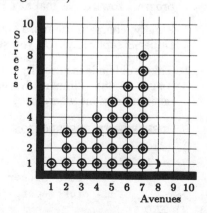

The Final Situation

Figure 5–15: A Sorting Task

CHAPTER SIX

ADVANCED
ROBOT PROGRAMMING

This chapter introduces two defined instructions, which we name zig-left-up and zag-down-right, that move Karel diagonally northwest and southeast respectively. Both of these instructions are defined by using only Karel's primitive instructions and turnright, but we derive immense conceptual power from being able to think in terms of Karel moving diagonally. With the aid of these diagonal-moving instructions, we shall propose and solve a set of novel beeper-manipulation programming problems. The student should be forewarned that although the new instructions in this chapter are small, the programming problems discussed are quite complex.

6.1 The zig-left-up and zag-down-right Instructions

The following definitions introduce the stars of this chapter: zig-left-up and zag-down-right. These direction pairs are not arbitrary; if Karel moves to the left and upward long enough, he eventually reaches the western boundary wall. The same argument holds for traveling down and toward the right, except that in this case Karel eventually reaches the southern boundary wall.

The other two possible direction pairs lack these useful properties: Karel will never find a boundary wall by traveling up and toward the right, and we cannot be sure which of the two boundary walls he will come upon first when traveling downward and to the left.

The following instructions define zig-left-up and zag-down-right.

```
DEFINE-NEW-INSTRUCTION zig-left-up AS
BEGIN
    move;
    turnright;
    move;
    turnleft
END
```

91

```
DEFINE-NEW-INSTRUCTION zag-down-right AS
BEGIN
  move;
  turnleft;
  move;
  turnright
END
```

Observe that no part of these instructions forces Karel to move in the intended directions. To execute zig-left-up correctly, Karel must be facing west; to execute zag-down-right correctly, Karel must be facing south. These requirements are called the <u>preconditions</u> of the instructions. A precondition of an instruction is a condition that must be made true before Karel can correctly execute the instruction. We have seen other examples of preconditions in this book, although we did not give them a special name until now.

For this example, the directional precondition of zig-left-up is that Karel is facing west; likewise, the directional precondition of zag-down-right is that Karel is facing south. Karel's execution of these instructions, when their preconditions are satisfied, is shown in Figure 6–1.

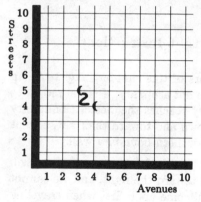
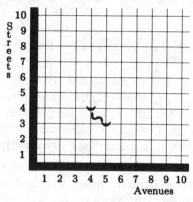

zig-left-up   zag-down-right

Figure 6–1: Execution of the Zig-Zag Instructions

Here is a statement that is loaded with terminology: the directional preconditions of zig-left-up and zag-down-right are invariant over each instruction's execution. This just means that if Karel is facing west and he executes zig-left-up, he still is facing west after the instruction has finished executing. This property allows Karel to execute a sequence of zig-left-ups without having to re-establish their directional precondition. A similar statement holds about Karel's facing south and zag-down-right. Also, observe that each instruction must be executed only when Karel's front is clear. This precondition is not invariant over the instructions, because Karel may be one block away from a corner where his front is blocked (for example, Karel may execute zig-left-up while facing west on the corner of 4th St. & 2nd Ave.).

6.2 Searching for a Beeper

The first major instruction that we write in this chapter solves the problem of finding a beeper that can be located anywhere in the world. Our task is to write an instruction named find-beeper that positions Karel on the same corner as a beeper. We have already seen one version of this problem (Problem 5.6–7), where both Karel and the beeper are in an enclosed room. The current formulation of this problem has less stringent restrictions: the beeper is placed on some arbitrary street corner in Karel's world, and there are no wall sections in the world. Of course, the boundary walls are always present.

One simple solution may spring to mind. In this attempted solution, Karel first goes to the origin and then faces east. He then moves eastward on 1st Street looking for a beeper. If Karel finds the beeper on 1st Street, he has accomplished his task; if he does not find the beeper on 1st Street, he moves back to the western boundary wall, switches over to 2nd Street, and continues searching from there. Karel repeats this strategy until he finds the beeper. Unfortunately, there is a mistaken assumption that is implicit in this search method: there is no way for Karel to know that the beeper is not on 1st Street. No matter how much of 1st Street Karel explores, he can never be sure that the beeper is not one block farther east.

It looks as if we and Karel are caught in an impossible trap, but there is an ingenious solution to our problem. As you might expect, it involves zig-zag moves. We need to program Karel to perform a radically different type of search pattern; Figure 6–2 shows such a pattern, and we use it below to define the find-beeper instruction.

This search method expands the search frontier in a manner similar to the way water would expand over Karel's world from an overflowing sink at the origin. Roughly, we can view Karel as traveling back and forth diagonally on the fringe of this water wave. Convince yourself that this search pattern is guaranteed to find the beeper eventually, regardless of the beeper's location—in our analogy, you need to convince yourself that the beeper will eventually get wet. We can use stepwise refinement to write the find-beeper instruction using this search method with the zig-left-up and zag-down-right instructions.

```
DEFINE-NEW-INSTRUCTION find-beeper AS
BEGIN
  go-to-origin;
  face-west;
  WHILE not-next-to-a-beeper DO
    IF facing-west
      THEN zig-move
      ELSE zag-move
END
```

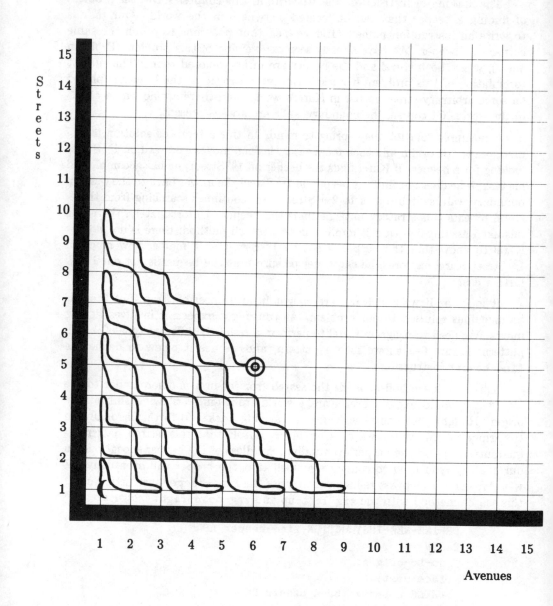

Figure 6–2: A Method for Searching Every Corner

The find-beeper instruction starts by moving Karel to the origin and then facing him west. These instructions establish the directional precondition for zig-left-up. The WHILE loop's purpose is to keep Karel moving until he finds a beeper, and by the formal WHILE property it is correct if the loop eventually terminates. The IF instruction, which is nested within the body of the loop, determines which direction Karel has been traveling and continues moving him along the diagonal in this same direction. We continue the stepwise refinement by writing zig-move and zag-move.

```
DEFINE-NEW-INSTRUCTION zig-move AS
BEGIN
  IF front-is-clear
    THEN zig-left-up
    ELSE advance-to-next-diagonal
END
```

and

```
DEFINE-NEW-INSTRUCTION zag-move AS
BEGIN
  IF front-is-clear
    THEN zag-down-right
    ELSE advance-to-next-diagonal
END
```

The moving instructions zig-move and zag-move operate similarly; therefore, we discuss only zig-move. When Karel is able to keep zigging, the zig-move instruction moves him diagonally to the next corner; otherwise, he is blocked by the western boundary wall and must advance northward to the next diagonal. We now write the instruction that advances Karel to the next diagonal.

```
DEFINE-NEW-INSTRUCTION advance-to-next-diagonal AS
BEGIN
  IF facing-west
    THEN turnright
    ELSE turnleft;
  move;
  turnaround
END
```

The advance-to-next-diagonal instruction starts by facing Karel away from the origin; he turns a different direction depending on whether he has been zigging or zagging. In either case, Karel then moves one corner farther away from the origin and turns around. If Karel has been zigging on the current diagonal, after he executes advance-to-next-diagonal he is positioned to continue by zagging on the next diagonal, and vice versa.

Observe that when Karel executes a zig-left-up or zag-down-right instruction, he must visit two corners; the first is visited temporarily, and the second is catty-corner from Karel's starting corner. When thinking about these instructions, we should ignore the intermediate corner and just remember that these instructions move Karel diagonally. Also, notice that the temporarily visited corner is guaranteed not to have a beeper on it, because it is part of the wave front that Karel visited while he was on the previous diagonal sweep.

Simulate Karel's execution of find-beeper in the sample situation in Figure 6–2 to acquaint yourself with its operation; try to get a feel for how all these instructions fit together to accomplish the task. Pay particularly close attention to the advance-to-next-diagonal instruction. Test find-beeper in the situation where the beeper is on the origin and in situations where the beeper is next to either boundary wall.

6.3 Doing Arithmetic with Karel

In this section we describe how Karel can be given addition problems and how we can program him to compute sums. Suppose that we want Karel to add the numbers 6 and 3. We can represent this problem in Karel's world by placing a beeper on the <u>question corner</u> of 6th St. & 3rd Ave. Karel's answer to this problem is represented by his putting down the beeper somewhere on 1st Street; the avenue that this beeper must be placed on is the sum of the two numbers being added. For this example, Karel should deposit the beeper on 1st St. & 9th Ave. We call this the <u>answer corner</u>. In general, if the question corner is S^{th} St. & A^{th} Ave. then the answer corner should be 1st St. & $(S + A)^{th}$ Ave.

This addition problem can be partitioned into two separate phases. In the first phase, Karel must locate the question corner and pick up the beeper. This phase can be accomplished by executing a find-beeper instruction followed by a pickbeeper instruction. During the second phase, Karel computes the sum of the two numbers and then puts the beeper down on the answer corner. We can naturally transcribe this plan into a program that solves the entire problem.

```
BEGINNING-OF-EXECUTION
    find-beeper;
    pickbeeper;
    compute-sum;
    putbeeper;
    turnoff
END-OF-EXECUTION
```

The sum can be computed by instructing Karel to zag down toward 1st Street. Before writing the compute-sum instruction, let's see why zagging helps to solve the problem. Assume that Karel has found the beeper on S^{th} St. & A^{th} Ave. By performing a zag-down-right instruction, he moves to the corner of $(S-1)^{st}$ St. & $(A+1)^{st}$ Ave. In our example, he moves from 6th St. & 3rd Ave. to 5th St.

4th Ave. This happens because the `zag-down-right` instruction decreases the street number that Karel is on by one (it moves him south by one block) and increases the avenue number that he is on by one (it moves him east one block).

The invariant during `compute-sum` is that the sum of the street number and the avenue number of Karel's position is always $S+A$ (that is, the sum is always equal to Karel's original street number plus his original avenue number). By executing a `zag-down-right` instruction, Karel preserves this invariant because of the following property of arithmetic.

$$S + A = (S - 1) + (A + 1)$$

If Karel continues performing `zag-down-right` instructions whenever his front is clear, he will repeatedly move south (and east) until he arrives at 1st Street. By continuing to subtract 1 from Karel's street number while adding 1 to Karel's avenue number, our invariant equation tells us that

$$S + A = (S - 1) + (A + 1) = (S - 2) + (A + 2) = \cdots = 1 + (A + S - 1)$$

Therefore, when Karel's street position decreases to 1, his avenue position will be $A + S - 1$. To complete the sum, all Karel must do is move one avenue to the east. He will then be on the answer corner of 1st St. & $(A + S)^{\text{th}}$ Ave. Karel's complete motion for the proposed example is illustrated in Figure 6-3.

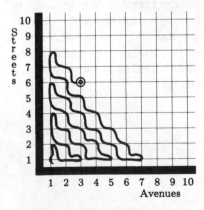

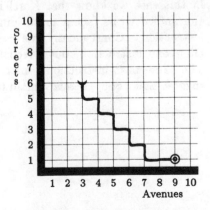

Find the Question Corner

Compute the Sum

Figure 6-3: The Two Phases of Computing a Sum

The definition for the compute-sum instruction is written below.

```
DEFINE-NEW-INSTRUCTION compute-sum AS
BEGIN
  face-south;
  WHILE front-is-clear DO
    zag-down-right;
  face-east;
  move
END
```

Why have we included a face-south instruction immediately before the WHILE loop? We must do so because the specifications for the find-beeper instruction say nothing about which direction Karel is facing when find-beeper finishes (in fact, sometimes he will be facing west and sometimes he will be facing south when find-beeper finishes). To satisfy the directional precondition for zag-down-right, we must guarantee that Karel is facing south before he begins executing the WHILE loop.

In general, programs that we write by using stepwise refinement are especially susceptible to bugs caused by unsatisfied preconditions. This type of error is initially very easy to overlook, so we must be careful and try to catch and correct unsatisfied precondition bugs as we develop our programs. As another example, in the room-escaping program (see pages 84-85) we had to command Karel to turn left immediately after he executed go-to-wall. This action is necessary because a precondition of the follow-until-door-is-on-right instruction is that Karel's right side must be blocked by a wall.

Along similar lines, what can we say about the face-east instruction? In this case we know that Karel has been correctly zagging; therefore, he is guaranteed to be facing south immediately before he executes the face-east instruction. Consequently, we can replace face-east in this instance by a turnleft instruction, but I recommend against performing this replacement. The face-east instruction is more descriptive than turnleft, and therefore I suggest that compute-sum remain in its present form.

6.4 Problem Set

Most of the following problems use combinations of the zig-left-up and zag-down-right instructions, or simple variants of these. Each problem is difficult to solve, but once a plan is discovered (probably through an "aha experience"), the program that implements the solution will not be too difficult to write. In all these problems, you may assume that find-beeper has already been defined, so you are not required to write its definition in your programs. You may also assume that there are no wall sections in the world. Finally, you should assume that Karel starts with no beepers in his beeper-bag, unless you are told otherwise. Do not make any assumptions about Karel's starting corner or starting direction, unless they are specified in the problem.

1. Rewrite both zig-left-up and zag-down-right so that they automatically satisfy their directional preconditions.

2. Assume that there is a beeper on 1st St. and N^{th} Ave. Program Karel to find it and then move it to N^{th} St. and 1st Ave.

▶3. Assume that there is a beeper on S^{th} St. & A^{th} Ave., and that Karel has two beepers in his bag. Program Karel to put the beepers from his bag on to 1st St. & A^{th} Ave. and S^{th} St. & 1st Ave. The original beeper must remain at the corner it starts on.

▶4. Assume that there is a beeper on 1st St. & A^{th} Ave. Program Karel to double the avenue number; he must move this beeper to 1st St. & $2A^{th}$ Ave. (For example, a beeper on 1st St. & 7th Ave. must be moved to 1st St. & 14th Ave.) **Hint:** Use the west boundary wall as in Problem 6.4-2.

5. Assume that Karel starts his task with an infinite number of beepers in his beeper-bag. Also assume that there is a beeper on 1st St. & N^{th} Ave. Program Karel to leave N beepers on the origin.

▶6. Assume that there is a beeper on S^{th} St. & 1st Ave. and a beeper on 1st St. & A^{th} Ave. Program Karel to put one of these beepers on S^{th} St. & A^{th} Ave. Karel must put the other beeper in his bag. **Hint:** There are many ways to plan this task. Here are two suggestions: (1) move one beeper south while moving the other beeper north; (2) continue moving one beeper until it is directly over (or to the right of) the stationary beeper. If done correctly, both methods will result in one beeper being placed on the answer corner.

7. Assume that Karel has a beeper in his beeper-bag and that there is another beeper on 1st St. & A^{th} Ave. Program Karel to place one of the beepers on 1st St. & 2^{Ath} Ave. This expression is 2 raised to the Ath power, or 1 doubled A times. For example, when A is 5, 2^A is 32. **Hint:** This problem uses instructions similar to those used to solve Problem 6.4–4. Karel can use the second beeper to count the number of times that he must double the number 1.

8. Repeat Problem 6.4–7, but this time the answer corner is 1st St. & 3^{Ath} Ave. Try to reuse as much of the previous program as possible.

▶9. Program Karel to place beepers in an outward spiral until his beeper-bag is empty. Assume that he will run out of beepers before he is stopped by the boundary walls. One example is shown is Figure 6–4.

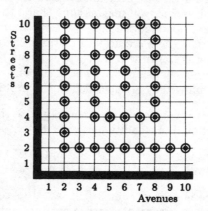

Figure 6–4: A Spiral

10. Assume that Karel has two beepers and that there is another beeper on S^{th} St. & A^{th} Ave. Program Karel to deposit one of these beepers on the corner of 1st St. & SA^{th} Ave. (This expression is S multiplied by A.)

11. Assume that Karel has three beepers and that there is another beeper on S^{th} St. & A^{th} Ave. Program Karel to deposit a beeper on the corner of 1st St. & S^{Ath} Ave. (This expression is S raised to the power of A).

12. Assume that Karel has three beepers in his beeper-bag and that there is another beeper on S^{th} St. & A^{th} Ave. Program Karel to put a beeper on the corner of 1st St. & GCD$(S,A)^{th}$ Ave. The GCD of two numbers is their Greatest Common Divisor. For example, the GCD of 6 and 15 is 3. **Hint:** Use Euclid's subtractive method.

13. Assume that Karel has N beepers in his beeper bag. Program him to place beepers on 1st Street and all the avenues that represent prime numbers between 1st Avenue and $N - \sqrt{N}^{th}$ Avenue.

14. If you enjoy computer science and eventually take a course in computability theory, fondly recall the days you spent programming Karel and try to solve the following problem: Prove that Karel, even without the aid of any beepers, is equivalent to a Turing machine. **Hint:** Use the equivalence between Turing machines and 2-counter automata. Remember that Karel's instructions are not mutually recursive, so state information must be encoded in some other manner.

ROBOT PROGRAMMING SUMMARY

Primitive Instructions

1) `move`   Karel moves one block forward.
2) `turnleft`   Karel pivots 90° to the left.
3) `pickbeeper` Karel puts a beeper in his beeper-bag.
4) `putbeeper`   Karel places a beeper on the corner.
5) `turnoff`   Karel turns himself off.

Block Structuring Instruction

```
6) BEGIN
      <instruction>;
      <instruction>;

         .        .
         .        .
         .        .

      <instruction>;
      <instruction>
   END
```

Conditional Instructions

```
7) IF <test>
      THEN <instruction>
```

```
8) IF <test>
      THEN <instruction>
      ELSE <instruction>
```

Repetition Instructions

```
9) ITERATE <positive-number> TIMES
      <instruction>
```

```
10) WHILE <test> DO
       <instruction>
```

The Mechanism for Defining New Instructions

11) DEFINE-NEW-INSTRUCTION <new-name> AS
    <instruction>

Specifying a Complete Program

12) BEGINNING-OF-PROGRAM

DEFINE-NEW-INSTRUCTION <new-name> AS
<instruction>;
        .
        .
        .
DEFINE-NEW-INSTRUCTION <new-name> AS
<instruction>;

BEGINNING-OF-EXECUTION
    <instruction>;
        .   .
        .   .
        .   .
    <instruction>
END-OF-EXECUTION
END-OF-PROGRAM

Bracketed Words

1) <instruction>   Any of the robot instructions (1-10)
2) <new-name>   Any new word (in lower-case letters, numbers, "-"
3) <positive-number>   Any positive number
4) <test>   Any of the following:
                                 front-is-clear, front-is-blocked,
                                 left-is-clear, left-is-blocked,
                                 right-is-clear, right-is-blocked,
                                 next-to-a-beeper, not-next-to-a-beeper,
                                 facing-north, not-facing-north,
                                 facing-south, not-facing-south,
                                 facing-east, not-facing-east,
                                 facing-west, not-facing-west,
                                 any-beepers-in-beeper-bag,
                                 no-beepers-in-beeper-bag

TECHNICAL TERM INDEX

INSTRUCTION INDEX

Instruction names followed by "(prob.)" have definitions that the reader is asked to write in the problem sets. Their numbers refer to the problems in which the specifications for the instructions are given.

106